CSA
Comprehension Strategy Assessment
Second Edition

Levels J–M/18–28

Grade 2

BENCHMARK EDUCATION COMPANY

Benchmark Education Company
145 Huguenot Street • New Rochelle, NY • 10801

Copyright © 2015 Benchmark Education Company, LLC. All rights reserved. The classroom teacher may reproduce the assessment and scoring pages in this teacher resource for individual classroom use only. The reproduction of any part of this teacher resource for an entire grade division, or entire school or school system, is strictly prohibited. No other part of this publication may be reproduced or transmitted in whole or in part in any form or by any means, electronic or mechanical, including photocopy, recording, or any information storage or retrieval system, without permission in writing from the publisher.

Common Core State Standards © Copyright 2010. National Governors Association Center for Best Practices and Council of Chief State School Officers. All rights reserved.
Printed in Guangzhou, China. 4401/0315/CA21401924

ISBN: 978-1-4900-6836-7

For ordering information, call Toll-Free 1-877-236-2465 or visit our Web site at www.benchmarkeducation.com.

Table of Contents

Introduction 4

Directions for Administering and Scoring Assessments 5

Pretest 10

Ongoing Comprehension Strategy Assessments 26

Ongoing Assessments Answer Key 28

Comprehension Strategies

    1–2   Analyze Character 32

    3–4   Analyze Story Elements 34

    5–6   Analyze Text Structure and Organization 36

    7–8   Compare and Contrast 38

    9–10 Evaluate Fact and Opinion 40

  11–12 Distinguish Real from Make-Believe 42

  13–14 Draw Conclusions 44

  15–16 Evaluate Author's Purpose 46

  17–18 Identify Cause and Effect 48

  19–20 Identify Main Idea and Supporting Details 50

  21–22 Identify Sequence of Events 52

  23–24 Make Inferences 54

  25–26 Make Predictions 56

  27–28 Summarize Information 58

  29–30 Use Graphic Features 60

  31–32 Use Text Features 62

Word Study Strategies

  33–34 Identify Synonyms, Antonyms, and Homonyms 64

  35–36 Use Context Clues to Determine Word Meaning 66

  37–38 Use Word Structures to Determine Word Meaning .. 68

Midyear Test 70

Posttest 86

    Answer Sheet 102

    Individual Scoring Charts 103

    Group Pretest/Midyear Test/Posttest Comparison Chart ... 106

    Ongoing Strategy Assessment Record 107

    Common Core State Standards and Virginia SOL Correlations 108

Introduction

The Comprehension Strategy Assessment book provides assessments for measuring students' grasp of comprehension strategies in both reading and listening. Information from these assessments can be used to support instruction. The passages are designed for students reading at Fluent Levels I–M.

This book contains three types of assessments:

- The **Pretest** is designed to assess students' reading comprehension strategies at the beginning of the school year. It provides a series of seven reading passages, both fiction and nonfiction, with a total of twenty-eight multiple-choice items. Information from the Pretest can be used to help plan instruction, make curriculum decisions, and select reading materials to match students' needs. Pretest scores can also be used as baseline data for evaluating students' progress from the beginning of the school year to the end.

- **Ongoing Comprehension Strategy Assessments** are focused two-page assessments to be administered periodically during the school year. Each assessment has a reading passage and a set of five test items to measure one specific strategy. There are two assessments per strategy, and they are intended to be used to monitor students' progress. They may be administered after completing instruction in particular strategies, or they may be administered at other appropriate times, such as the end of each grading period. These pages may be used as reading assessments or listening assessments.

- The Midyear and Posttests are parallel to the Pretest. They have the same number of reading passages and items as the Pretest, and test the same strategies. The **Midyear Test** can be administered as a formative assessment. The results can be used to adjust instruction to improve student learning. The **Posttest** is designed to be administered at the end of the school year as a final evaluation of students' progress in comparison to their performance at the beginning of the year.

The next few pages in this book provide directions for administering and scoring the assessments and using the assessment results. Answer keys for the Pretest, Ongoing Assessments, and Posttest can be found at the beginning of each section in this book. Scoring Charts for scoring the assessments and recording results can be found on pages 103–105.

DIRECTIONS FOR ADMINISTERING AND SCORING ASSESSMENTS

All of the assessments in this book may be administered to students individually or in a group. We recommend administering the Pretest, Midyear Test, and Posttest to all students at the same time. The Ongoing Comprehension Strategy Assessments may be administered in the same way, or they may be administered individually or in small groups to different students at different times. Detailed guidelines for administering and scoring each type of assessment follow.

GUIDELINES FOR USING THE PRETEST

The Pretest is fourteen pages long. Included are seven, one-page reading passages and a set of multiple-choice questions for each passage: twenty-eight items total. These twenty-eight items measure seven "clusters" of strategies and skills (as listed on the Individual Pretest Scoring Chart, page 103) with four items per cluster. Each cluster has two or three strategies grouped by similarities. For example, "Identify Main Idea and Supporting Details" and "Summarize Information" are grouped together in one cluster because they involve similar thinking skills (distinguishing essential from inessential information). Each cluster has been labeled with a title that reflects the key thinking skill, such as "Distinguishing Important Information."

Plan for about 60 minutes to administer the Pretest, but allow more time if needed. Students should be allowed to answer every question. Depending on the students and your situation, you may want to administer the Pretest in two parts in different sittings.

To Administer the Pretest:

1. Make a copy of the test and Answer Sheet for each student.
2. Instruct students to write their names and the date at the top of each test page.
3. Read the directions on the first page and make sure students understand what to do.
4. Instruct students to read each passage and answer the questions that go with it.
5. For each multiple-choice question, instruct students to choose the best answer and fill in the bubble beside the answer they choose.
6. When students have finished, collect the tests and Answer Sheets.

To Score the Pretest:

1. Make a copy of the Individual Pretest Scoring Chart (see page 103) for each student.

2. Refer to the Pretest Answer Key on page 11. It gives the letter of the correct response to each question.

3. Mark each question correct or incorrect on the test page.

4. To find the total test score, count the number of items answered correctly.

5. To score by cluster, use the Individual Pretest Scoring Chart. At the top of the chart, circle the number of each item answered correctly. The item numbers are organized by clusters of tested skills.

6. For each cluster on the scoring chart, add the number of items answered correctly (for example, 3 of 4). Write the number correct in the right-hand column under Pretest Score.

Using the Results:

1. Use the results of the Pretest to determine each student's current level of reading ability, as well as his or her proficiencies in the strategies being tested.

2. As explained above, the items in the Pretest measure strategies in particular clusters. A student's score on a particular cluster can pinpoint specific instructional needs. A student who answers two or more items in a skill cluster incorrectly may need focused instructional attention on those particular strategies.

3. The Individual Scoring Charts and Group Pretest/Midyear Test/Posttest Comparison Chart provide handy references for monitoring students' growth and development. Such information can be used to identify the skills and strategies to be reinforced for a whole group, a small group, or an individual.

4. Store the Individual Scoring Charts for the Pretest, Midyear Test, and Posttest in an appropriate location for referral during the school year, and for end-of-year comparison of the Pretest and Posttest scores.

GUIDELINES FOR USING THE ONGOING COMPREHENSION STRATEGY ASSESSMENTS

In this program, Fluent Level Grade 2 covers nineteen comprehension and word study strategies in seven skill clusters. In this book, you will find two assessments for each strategy (arranged in alphabetical order by strategy within Comprehension Skills and Word Study Skills). The assessments are numbered 1–38. Each assessment is one page.

The purpose of these assessments is to determine how well students have learned each strategy. You may want to administer the two strategy-based assessments at set times of the year (such as during the second and third quarters), or you can administer an assessment for a specific strategy just after teaching the strategy in the classroom. In some cases, you may want to administer both of the assessments for a particular strategy at the same time. Although the assessments are numbered sequentially 1–38, they do not need to be administered in any set order. You may assess strategies according to the order in which you choose to teach them.

Each Ongoing Comprehension Strategy Assessment consists of a reading passage and two questions. The two questions are multiple choice.

Plan for about 10–15 minutes to administer an Ongoing Comprehension Strategy Assessment but allow more time if needed.

To Administer an Ongoing Assessment:

1. Make a copy of the assessment for each student.

2. Instruct students to write their names and the date at the top of each test page.

3. Direct students to read each passage and answer the questions that go with it.

4. For each multiple-choice question, instruct students to choose the best answer and fill in the bubble beside the answer they choose.

5. For short-answer questions, instruct students to write their responses (in phrases and complete sentences) on the lines provided.

Listening Comprehension

Ongoing Assessments 1–32 are intended primarily for use as written assessments of reading comprehension. However, they may also be used as measures of listening comprehension. To use them for listening purposes, read the passage aloud to the student(s) and ask the student(s) to answer the questions. Students may respond by marking and writing their answers on the test page, or you may direct students to give oral responses. If preferred, you may use one of the two Ongoing Assessments for reading comprehension and the other for listening.

To Score an Ongoing Assessment:

1. Refer to the appropriate Answer Key (on pages 28–31). The answer key gives the letter of the correct response for each multiple-choice question.

2. Mark each question correct or incorrect on the test page.

3. To find the total score, count the number of items answered correctly.

Using the Results:

1. Use the results of the Ongoing Assessment to evaluate each student's understanding of the tested strategy or skill.

2. A student who understands and applies a given strategy should answer both items correctly—or 3 out of 4 questions on the two assessments combined. A student who answers only one or none of the items may need additional instruction on a particular strategy.

3. Use the Ongoing Strategy Assessment Record to keep track of a student's scores on the assessments during the school year. The record provides space for writing the score on each of the two strategy assessments.

GUIDELINES FOR USING THE MIDYEAR AND POSTTESTS

The Midyear and Posttests have the same number of reading passages and items as the Pretest and should be administered and scored in the same way. The items on these tests measure the same skills as the Pretest with the same number of items in each skill cluster. Thus, students' scores on the three tests can be compared using the Group Pretest/Midyear Test/Posttest Comparison Chart on page 106.

Use the results of the Midyear Test to pinpoint specific instructional needs. A student who answers two or more items in a skill cluster incorrectly may need focused instructional attention on those particular comprehension or word study strategies.

Use the results of the Posttest to determine each student's current level of reading ability, as well as his or her proficiencies in the strategies being tested. Compare the student's scores on the Pretest and Posttest—and on each strategy cluster within the tests—to evaluate the student's progress since the beginning of the year.

COMPREHENSION STRATEGY ASSESSMENTS ONLINE

The Comprehension Strategy Assessments are also available online. The online tests can be administered on any device, including desktop computers, laptops, and tablets. They give students valuable experience with online testing, and offer teachers robust data-driven assessment with reporting by classroom, grade, school, and district.

Pretest

The Travelers and the Bear 12

Pioneer Children at Work 14

Ready to Ride 16

Acting Like a Child 18

Clouds 20

The Cardinals 22

Rabbit or Hare? 24

Pretest Answer Key

1. A
2. B
3. C
4. C
5. A
6. C
7. B
8. B
9. B
10. C
11. B
12. A
13. A
14. C
15. C
16. B
17. A
18. A
19. C
20. B
21. B
22. A
23. C
24. C
25. B
26. B
27. C
28. A

The Travelers and the Bear

One day long ago, two friends were traveling together. Their path led them into a deep forest. All of a sudden, a big bear rushed at the men. The bear was hungry and looking for a meal.

One of the men ran to a tree. He quickly climbed it and hid in the branches. The bear could not see him.

The other man was not so lucky. The bear was so close he could not get away. But the man knew what to do. He dropped to the ground and pretended to be dead. He did not even breathe. The bear walked around the man. Then he sniffed the man's face and rubbed his nose against the man's ear. At last the bear walked off, <u>certain</u> that the man was dead.

After the bear was safely gone, the first man jumped down from the tree. He hurried to his friend and asked, "What did that bear whisper to you just now?"

"Oh," said the second man. "He told me never to travel with a friend who thinks only of himself when danger is near."

Name _____ Date _____

1. What were the two friends doing in this story?
   Ⓐ traveling through a forest
   Ⓑ looking for food to eat
   Ⓒ resting under a tree

2. Which word best describes the second man?
   Ⓐ strange
   Ⓑ clever
   Ⓒ lazy

3. The story says, "Then the bear walked away, certain that the man was dead." Which word means the same as certain?
   Ⓐ happy
   Ⓑ worried
   Ⓒ sure

4. Which of these could NOT really happen?
   Ⓐ A bear rushes at two men.
   Ⓑ A man pretends to be dead.
   Ⓒ A bear whispers to a man.

Name _____ Date _____

Directions: Read the passage. Then use the information from the passage to answer questions 5–8.

Pioneer Children at Work

In pioneer days, many children did not go to school. But these children did not play much either. They had many jobs. They worked hard every day.

Every pioneer family had a garden. The children helped in the garden. They planted seeds and picked the crops.

The family raised animals. Young children fed the chickens and gathered their eggs. Older children milked the cows. They helped cut the sheep's wool.

Some jobs were mostly for girls. They learned to sew and cook. They washed clothes. They made candles and soap.

Boys had many outdoor jobs. They <u>repaired</u> broken fences. They helped build barns. In time, they learned to hunt.

Life was not easy for pioneer children. But they learned many skills. When they grew up, they passed the skills on to their own children.

Name _____   Date _____

5. What is the main idea of this passage?
- Ⓐ Pioneer children worked hard every day.
- Ⓑ Every pioneer family had a garden.
- Ⓒ A pioneer family raised animals.

6. What is paragraph 4 mostly about?
- Ⓐ learning to sew
- Ⓑ the work of pioneer children
- Ⓒ jobs done by girls

7. The passage says, "They repaired broken fences." What does repaired mean?
- Ⓐ climbed
- Ⓑ fixed
- Ⓒ cleaned

8. The author wrote this passage to _____.
- Ⓐ Show that hard work can be fun.
- Ⓑ Describe how pioneer children lived.
- Ⓒ Tell a funny story about pioneer children.

Name _____ Date _____

Directions: Read the passage. Then use the information from the passage to answer questions 9–12.

Ready to Ride

The sun was shining, and the air was warm. It was a perfect day for the first bike ride of the year. "How about it, Dad?" asked Jada. "We could ride to the creek and back. All the trees are in bloom. It will be such a pretty ride!"

Dad frowned. "That's a long uphill ride on the way home. It might be a little too much for us on the first time out."

"Maybe for you," Jada teased. "But I'm in great shape." With that, she ran out to the garage. She wheeled out her bike and strapped on her helmet. Then she began to pedal up and down the long dirt driveway.

Jada came back inside after five minutes. She was huffing and puffing. "Maybe I'm not in such good shape after all!" she began. "I can hardly pedal around the driveway."

Dad just laughed. "The problem is your bike, not you. Your tires went flat. It happened when the weather was cold."

Then Dad led Jada back out to the garage. He found his air pump hanging from a wall hook. "This will do the trick," he said.

Name _____ Date _____

9. What will happen next in the story?
  Ⓐ Dad and Jada will ride their bikes to the creek.
  Ⓑ Dad will pump air into the tires on Jada's bike.
  Ⓒ Dad and Jada will go for a ride in the car.

10. What problem did Jada have in this story?
  Ⓐ Her bike was too small for her.
  Ⓑ She did not like to ride uphill.
  Ⓒ Her bike's tires were flat.

11. What season is it in this story?
  Ⓐ winter
  Ⓑ spring
  Ⓒ fall

12. The author's purpose in this passage is to _____.
  Ⓐ tell a story about a girl and her father
  Ⓑ teach children how to ride bikes
  Ⓒ describe a good place for a bike ride

Acting Like a Child

You probably don't know Karan Brar. But you may have seen him a few times. That's because Karan is a child <u>actor</u>. He acts in movies and on TV.

Karan was born in 1999. He is Indian American and speaks both English and Punjabi. He has a cute smile. For years, Karan has worked in front of a camera. He started by acting in TV ads. Then in 2010, he got a part in *Diary of a Wimpy Kid*. It was a big hit. Karan plays a classmate and friend of the main character, Greg Heffley.

Now Karan wants to keep acting. He has been a guest star on TV shows. He has made more movies, too. So keep your eyes open for Karan Brar. You'll probably be seeing a lot more of him.

Name _____ Date _____

13. This passage mostly tells about _____.
  Ⓐ events in time order
  Ⓑ how two things are alike
  Ⓒ how to make something

14. Which sentence is an opinion?
  Ⓐ Karan was born in 1999.
  Ⓑ He acts in movies and on TV.
  Ⓒ He has a cute smile.

15. What can you tell about Karan Brar?
  Ⓐ He does not enjoy going to school.
  Ⓑ He thinks movies are a waste of time.
  Ⓒ He likes making movies and TV shows.

16. What does <u>actor</u> mean?
  Ⓐ act again
  Ⓑ someone who acts
  Ⓒ a place for acting

Clouds

Clouds are fun to watch, but how much do you know about them? Here are some answers to questions you might have about clouds.

What is a cloud?

Some clouds look like puffs of cotton. Others look like blankets. But clouds are really made of tiny drops of water. Clouds are so light that they float in the air.

What makes rain fall from clouds?

Sometimes the drops of water in a cloud join together. The drops get larger and heavier. If they get heavy enough, they can't float anymore. The water drops fall to the ground as rain.

Are all clouds alike?

No, there are many kinds of clouds, and they have different shapes. Some clouds make rain, and some don't. Some form high in the sky, and some are low. The picture below shows the height of some clouds.

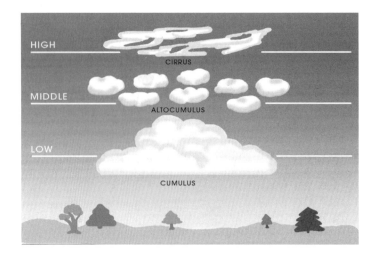

Name _____ Date _____

17. Which is the best summary of this passage?
- Ⓐ Clouds are made of water. Sometimes rain falls from clouds. There are many kinds of clouds.
- Ⓑ Clouds make rain. Some clouds float.
- Ⓒ Clouds float in the air. They look like cotton puffs. They look like blankets.

18. What part of the passage tells what clouds are made of?
- Ⓐ **What is a cloud?**
- Ⓑ **What makes rain fall from clouds?**
- Ⓒ **Are all clouds alike?**

19. Which word describes the height of the cirrus cloud?
- Ⓐ low
- Ⓑ middle
- Ⓒ high

20. Which of these clouds is in the "middle" of the sky?
- Ⓐ cirrus
- Ⓑ altocumulus
- Ⓒ cumulus

The Cardinals

"Come quickly, Ruby," said Mom. "A pair of cardinals is building a nest."

I went to the window where Mom was standing. A bright red bird was hopping across the lawn. It was small and quick. Over and over, the bird picked up small twigs with its beak. It flew off to our lilac bush with each twig, and then it returned to the lawn for another one.

Soon I saw a brown bird doing the same thing. "What kind of bird is that?" I asked.

"That's a cardinal, too," Mom explained. "The male is red, but the female is brown. Her dull color helps keep her safe while she sits on her eggs."

I watched the birds for a long while. They were beautiful, and I wanted them to feel welcome. Mom must have read my mind. "Let's go to the store, Ruby," she said. "We'll buy some sunflower seeds for our bird feeder."

Name _____ Date _____

21. What happened first in this story?
- Ⓐ Ruby looked out the window.
- Ⓑ Mom called Ruby to the window.
- Ⓒ Mom and Ruby went to the store.

22. Which clue tells you that the cardinals were building a nest?
- Ⓐ They were taking twigs to the bush.
- Ⓑ They were eating seeds.
- Ⓒ They were hopping across the lawn.

23. How is the male cardinal different from the female?
- Ⓐ His body is smaller.
- Ⓑ He spends more time in the nest.
- Ⓒ His color is brighter.

24. Why did Mom and Ruby decide to buy sunflower seeds?
- Ⓐ to have a snack
- Ⓑ to grow flowers
- Ⓒ to make the birds feel welcome

Name _____ Date _____

Directions: Read the passage. Then use the information from the passage to answer questions 25–28.

Rabbit or Hare?

Rabbits and hares are much alike. Both rabbits and hares have long ears and little tails. Both have short front legs and strong back legs, and both are very fast. They can hop away from danger at top speed.

Rabbits and hares are pretty animals, but farmers do not like them because they eat many kinds of plants. Farmers work hard to keep them out of their fields.

Rabbits and hares are different, too. Hares are bigger than rabbits, and their ears are longer. Baby hares have fur, and they can see when they are born. But baby rabbits are born blind, and they don't have fur at first.

How do rabbits and hares live? Rabbits make burrows under the ground and live in big groups. Hares make nests on the ground, and they don't live in groups. Hares <u>prefer</u> to live alone.

Name _____ Date _____

25. How are rabbits different from hares?
- Ⓐ Rabbits have short front legs.
- Ⓑ Rabbits are born blind.
- Ⓒ Rabbits have little tails.

26. Which sentence is a fact?
- Ⓐ Rabbits are pretty animals.
- Ⓑ Rabbits and hares eat plants.
- Ⓒ Rabbits make great pets.

27. The passage says, "They can hop away from danger at top speed." Which sentence has the same meaning?
- Ⓐ Their speed makes them dangerous.
- Ⓑ They can get hurt when they hop fast.
- Ⓒ They can quickly get away from danger.

28. The passage says, "Hares prefer to live alone." What does prefer mean?
- Ⓐ like
- Ⓑ play
- Ⓒ help

Ongoing Assessments

Assessment 1: **Annie Oakley, Shooting Star (Biography)** 32
Analyze Character

Assessment 2: **A Hero Named Jackie Robinson (Biography)** 33
Analyze Character

Assessment 3: **Belling the Cat (Fable)** 34
Analyze Story Elements

Assessment 4: **The Treasure Map (Realistic Fiction)** 35
Analyze Story Elements

Assessment 5: **Oceans of the World (Science Informational Text)** 36
Analyze Text Structure and Organization

Assessment 6: **The Ice Cream Story (Social Studies Informational Text)** 37
Analyze Text Structure and Organization

Assessment 7: **Cats and Dogs (Informational Article)** 38
Compare and Contrast

Assessment 8: **Big Cities, Small Towns (Social Studies Informational Text)** 39
Compare and Contrast

Assessment 9: **Turtles (Science Informational Text)** 40
Evaluate Fact and Opinion

Assessment 10: **Why I Love Trees (Science Informational Text)** 41
Evaluate Fact and Opinion

Assessment 11: **Paul Bunyan and Babe (Tall Tale)** 42
Distinguish Real from Make-Believe

Assessment 12: **The Lion and the Mouse (Fable)** 43
Distinguish Real from Make-Believe

Assessment 13: **Ants and Their Ways (Science Informational Text)** 44
Draw Conclusions

Assessment 14: **How Seeds Travel (Science Informational Text)** 45
Draw Conclusions

Assessment 15: **Tropical Fish Tanks (How-To Article)** 46
Evaluate Author's Purpose

Assessment 16: **Sailing Ships (Social Studies Informational Text)** 47
Evaluate Author's Purpose

Assessment 17: **Germs (Science Informational Text)** 48
Identify Cause and Effect

Assessment 18: **Making Bread (How-To Article)** 49
Identify Cause and Effect

Assessment 19: **Earthworms (Science Informational Text)** 50
Identify Main Idea and Supporting Details

Assessment 20: Buckle Up! (Informational Article) 51
Identify Main Idea and Supporting Details

Assessment 21: How Cider Is Made (Informational Article) 52
Identify Sequence of Events

Assessment 22: Mr. Willis and His Bricks (Informational Article) 53
Identify Sequence of Events

Assessment 23: A Special Day (Realistic Fiction) 54
Make Inferences

Assessment 24: Pretty as a Pearl (Informational Article) 55
Make Inferences

Assessment 25: Monkey Business (Science Informational Text) 56
Make Predictions

Assessment 26: Jake's Tree House (Realistic Fiction) 57
Make Predictions

Assessment 27: Along the Nile (Social Studies Informational Text) 58
Summarize Information

Assessment 28: Beetles (Science Informational Text) 59
Summarize Information

Assessment 29: How to Make "Bees" (How-To Article) 60
Use Graphic Features

Assessment 30: Animal Houses (Science Informational Text) 61
Use Graphic Features

Assessment 31: Did Your Clothes Grow? (Social Studies Informational Text) 62
Use Text Features

Assessment 32: Fun with Pine Cones (How-To Article) 63
Use Text Features

Assessment 33: Sweeping to a Win (Sports Article) 64
Identify Synonyms, Antonyms, and Homonyms

Assessment 34: How to Be Healthy and Strong (Science Informational Text) .. 65
Identify Synonyms, Antonyms, and Homonyms

Assessment 35: A World of Color (Informational Article) 66
Use Context Clues to Determine Word Meaning

Assessment 36: Clowning Around (Informational Article) 67
Use Context Clues to Determine Word Meaning

Assessment 37: Your First Aquarium (Informational Article) 68
Use Word Structures to Determine Word Meaning

Assessment 38: Good Queen Bess (Biography) 69
Use Word Structures to Determine Word Meaning

Ongoing Assessments Answer Key

Assessment 1: Annie Oakley, Shooting Star
(Analyze Character)
1. C
2. B

Assessment 2: A Hero Named Jackie Robinson
(Analyze Character)
1. B
2. C

Assessment 3: Belling the Cat
(Analyze Story Elements)
1. B
2. A

Assessment 4: The Treasure Map
(Analyze Story Elements)
1. C
2. B

Assessment 5: Oceans of the World
(Analyze Text Structure and Organization)
1. A
2. B

Assessment 6: The Ice Cream Story
(Analyze Text Structure and Organization)
1. A
2. C

Assessment 7: Cats and Dogs
(Compare and Contrast)
1. B
2. C

Assessment 8: Big Cities, Small Towns
(Compare and Contrast)
1. A
2. B

Assessment 9: Turtles
(Evaluate Fact and Opinion)
1. B
2. C

Assessment 10: Why I Love Trees
(Evaluate Fact and Opinion)
1. C
2. A

Assessment 11: Paul Bunyan and Babe
(Distinguish Real from Make-Believe)
1. B
2. C

Assessment 12: The Lion and the Mouse
(Distinguish Real from Make-Believe)
1. C
2. A

Assessment 13: Ants and Their Ways
(Draw Conclusions)
1. C
2. A

Assessment 14: How Seeds Travel
(Draw Conclusions)
1. B
2. C

Assessment 15: Tropical Fish Tanks
(Evaluate Author's Purpose)
1. C
2. B

Assessment 16: Sailing Ships
(Evaluate Author's Purpose)
1. A
2. B

Assessment 17: Germs
(Identify Cause and Effect)
1. B
2. A

Assessment 18: Making Bread
(Identify Cause and Effect)
1. A
2. C

Assessment 19: Earthworms
(Identify Main Idea and Supporting Details)
1. A
2. C

Assessment 20: Buckle Up!
(Identify Main Idea and Supporting Details)
1. B
2. A

Assessment 21: How Cider Is Made
(Identify Sequence of Events)
1. C
2. A

Assessment 22: Mr. Willis and His Bricks
(Identify Sequence of Events)
1. B
2. C

Assessment 23: A Special Day
(Make Inferences)
1. B
2. A

Assessment 24: Pretty as a Pearl
(Make Inferences)
1. C
2. B

Assessment 25: Monkey Business
(Make Predictions)
1. C
2. B

Assessment 26: Jake's Tree House
(Make Predictions)
1. A
2. C

Assessment 27: Along the Nile
(Summarize Information)
1. B
2. C

Assessment 28: Beetles
(Summarize Information)
1. C
2. B

Assessment 29: How to Make "Bees"
(Use Graphic Features)
1. C
2. A

Assessment 30: Animal Houses
(Use Graphic Features)
1. A
2. C

Assessment 31: Did Your Clothes Grow?
(Use Text Features)
1. A
2. B

Assessment 32: Fun with Pine Cones
(Use Text Features)
1. C
2. A

Assessment 33: Sweeping to a Win
(Identify Synonyms, Antonyms, and Homonyms)
1. C
2. B

Assessment 34: How to Be Healthy and Strong
(Identify Synonyms, Antonyms, and Homonyms)
1. A
2. C

Assessment 35: A World of Color
(Use Context Clues to Determine Word Meaning)
1. A
2. B

Assessment 36: Clowning Around
(Use Context Clues to Determine Word Meaning)
1. C
2. A

Assessment 37: Your First Aquarium
(Use Word Structures to Determine Word Meaning)
1. A
2. C

Assessment 38: Good Queen Bess
(Use Word Structures to Determine Word Meaning)
1. C
2. B

Ongoing Comprehension Strategy Assessment • 1

Name _____ Date _____

Directions: Read the passage. Then use the information from the passage to answer questions 1–2.

Annie Oakley, Shooting Star

Long before TV, Annie Oakley was a star.

Annie started out poor. She was born in 1860. She lived on a farm in Ohio. At age eight, she learned to shoot. Soon she began making money as a hunter. She paid for her family's farm.

In 1875, Annie entered a shooting match with Frank Butler. He was a great shooter, but Annie won. Frank did not get mad. Instead he fell in love. Soon Frank and Annie got married. Before long, they joined a Wild West show.

One of Annie's tricks was to lie on her back next to three guns. Frank threw six glass balls into the air. Annie grabbed a gun. Then she grabbed another. Each time she hit a ball in the air.

Kings and queens watched Annie's show. The poor farm girl became a big star.

1. Annie paid for her family's farm. What does this show about her?
   Ⓐ She always had lots of money.
   Ⓑ She loved animals.
   Ⓒ She cared about her family.

2. How did Annie become a star?
   Ⓐ She spent lots of money.
   Ⓑ She used her talent.
   Ⓒ She got help from Frank.

Name _____ Date _____

Directions: Read the passage. Then use the information from the passage to answer questions 1–2.

A Hero Named Jackie Robinson

Jackie Robinson was born in 1919. He was a black man and a baseball player. In those days, life was hard for blacks. They could not eat in some places. They had to sit at the back of buses. And black ball players could not play on white teams.

But that changed in 1947. Jackie Robinson joined the Dodgers. All the other players were white.

It was hard for Jackie at first. Some of the players on his team were not nice to him and did not want to play on the same team. Some players tried to hurt him. Fans shouted mean things.

But Jackie did not say a word. He just played ball, and he was great. He helped his team to win. The Dodgers went to the World Series that year. They won the Series in 1955.

Jackie Robinson died in 1972. By then, blacks had more rights. They did not have to sit at the back of a bus. They could eat anyplace. And, thanks to Jackie, many blacks got to play baseball.

1. Which words best describe Jackie Robinson?
   Ⓐ kind and nice
   Ⓑ strong and hardworking
   Ⓒ funny and interesting

2. What did Jackie do when people were mean to him?
   Ⓐ He quit playing ball.
   Ⓑ He shouted at them.
   Ⓒ He stayed quiet and calm.

Belling the Cat

Once upon a time, several mice lived in a farmhouse. It was a very fine place to live. There was always plenty of food, and it was warm in winter.

Then one day, the farmer and his wife got a new cat. It was a large, black cat with white paws, and it loved to hunt for mice. That cat moved into the house and guarded the food. No mouse could go anywhere safely anymore, and they started to get very hungry.

All the mice got together to decide what to do. One of the older mice said, "We must do something about this cat or we will starve."

Another mouse said, "We could move to a new house."

Then a young mouse stood up and said, "I know what to do. We will put a bell around the cat's neck. Then when the cat comes running to catch us, we will hear the bell. We can quickly escape."

The other mice cheered. This was a wonderful plan. But then a very old and very wise mouse stood up. "I have just one question," said the old mouse. "Who shall put the bell on the cat?"

No one had an answer for that.

1. Where does this story take place?
   Ⓐ in a city
   Ⓑ on a farm
   Ⓒ in the forest

2. What happened at the end of the story?
   Ⓐ The mice had a meeting.
   Ⓑ A cat moved into the house.
   Ⓒ The farmer got a bell.

Ongoing Comprehension Strategy Assessment • 4

Name _____ Date _____

Directions: Read the passage. Then use the information from the passage to answer questions 1–2.

The Treasure Map

On Monday, Stacey asked her friend Belle to come over to her house and play. After school, they took the bus together.

"What will we play?" asked Belle when they got to Stacey's room.

"Let's play pirates," said Stacey. "You can be Captain Claw, and I'll be Redbeard."

The girls went to the living room and made the sofa into a pirate ship. Belle stood at the front as a lookout. Stacey stood near the back and waved her play sword.

Then Stacey's mother came into the room. She was holding a piece of paper. "I have just found a map," she said, smiling. "It seems to show the way to a hidden treasure."

"Wow," said Stacey, "let's find it!"

The girls followed the map to the kitchen. They spotted an X under the kitchen table and a box on the floor. Belle quickly opened the box, and there was the treasure! They found two peanut butter and jelly sandwiches and two chocolate milks.

"Now that's a good treasure," said Stacey as they sat down to eat.

1. Where does the story take place?
    Ⓐ Belle's house
    Ⓑ on a ship
    Ⓒ Stacey's house

2. Why did Stacey's mom give the girls a map?
    Ⓐ The girls were looking for a hidden treasure.
    Ⓑ The map showed the girls where to find a snack.
    Ⓒ Mom wanted the girls to quit playing pirate.

Oceans of the World

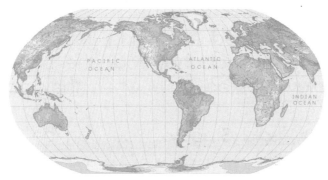

Most of Earth is covered by water. There are four oceans on Earth. They are all connected together.

1 _____

The oceans are full of life. Many plants grow in the oceans. There are many kinds of animals, too, such as fish and crabs. The biggest animal in the world lives in the ocean. It is the blue whale. It can grow to more than 110 feet long.

2 _____

All parts of the ocean are not the same. Some parts are cold, and some are warm. Some parts are very deep. Some parts have mountains. In fact, the tallest mountain on Earth is in the ocean.

1. What title fits best on line 1?
   Ⓐ Ocean Life
   Ⓑ Sea Animals
   Ⓒ Many Plants

2. What title fits best on line 2?
   Ⓐ Mountains
   Ⓑ Parts of the Ocean
   Ⓒ Deep Places

Ongoing Comprehension Strategy Assessment • 6

Name _____ Date _____

Directions: Read the passage. Then use the information from the passage to answer questions 1–2.

The Ice Cream Story

How old is ice cream? Who made it first? No one knows for sure. Long ago, people put honey on snow to make a cool treat. Later, people began to mix fruit and ice.

Ice cream was made in Italy in the 1600s. Soon, people made ice cream in France and Germany. In the 1700s, ice cream came to America for the first time.

In 1851, a man named Jacob Fussell was selling milk. Then he found that he could make ice cream from milk. He built the first ice cream factory in America.

But what is ice cream without a cone? The first cones were made in 1904. Since then, we have found many ways to make and eat ice cream.

1. This passage is organized by _____.
   - Ⓐ time order
   - Ⓑ cause and effect
   - Ⓒ same/different

2. What did Jacob Fussell do in 1851?
   - Ⓐ He invented the ice cream cone.
   - Ⓑ He made the first ice cream in Italy.
   - Ⓒ He built the first ice cream factory in America.

Name _____ Date _____

Directions: Read the passage. Then use the information from the passage to answer questions 1–2.

Cats and Dogs

Cats and dogs make good pets. They get along well with people and are good with children. You can keep many kinds of cats and dogs in the house, and they are not too messy.

Some cats and dogs are not just pets. They work. For example, house cats are good at hunting. They can keep pests away, so many farmers keep cats to catch mice. Some dogs also work on farms. For example, sheepdogs and collies can protect sheep, hens, and other animals.

Working dogs have many other jobs. "Seeing eye" dogs help blind people. They take them to work and help them get around. Dogs also help keep people safe by watching houses and guarding stores. Other dogs work on TV and in movies, and some cats do, too.

1. **How are cats and dogs the same?**
   Ⓐ Cats and dogs keep people safe.
   Ⓑ Cats and dogs get along with people.
   Ⓒ Cats and dogs are good at hunting.

2. **What is one way dogs are different from cats?**
   Ⓐ Dogs work on farms.
   Ⓑ Dogs are good with children.
   Ⓒ Some dogs help blind people.

Name _____ Date _____

Directions: Read the passage. Then use the information from the passage to answer questions 1–2.

Big Cities, Small Towns

Do you like big cities? Many people live and work in big cities. Big cities are fun to visit. They have many stores for shopping and loads of places to eat. Cities offer many things to see and do. They have tall buildings and many streets.

Most big cities are loud because there is so much traffic. People are on the move. Cars fill the streets, and buses and trains carry people back and forth.

Do you like small towns? People live and work in small towns, too, but small towns are not as noisy as cities. They are not as busy or crowded. Small towns do not have as many streets or cars or buses, and the buildings are not as tall.

People stop and talk in small towns. They know their neighbors, and they walk from their houses into town. They do not need taxis and trains. Small towns are fun to visit, too.

1. How are big cities and small towns the same?
Ⓐ They are fun to visit.
Ⓑ They have many streets.
Ⓒ They do not need trains.

2. How are small towns different than big cities?
Ⓐ Small towns have more tall buildings.
Ⓑ Small towns are not as noisy.
Ⓒ Small towns are more crowded.

Turtles

Everyone knows that turtles have shells, and they move rather slowly. Spotted turtles and mud turtles like to live in ponds. Box turtles and painted turtles spend more time on land.

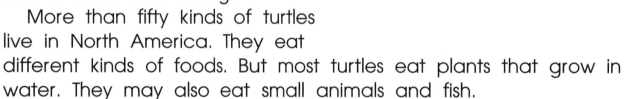

Most kinds of turtles can pull their head and tail inside their shell. It keeps the turtle safe. The shell is hard and strong.

More than fifty kinds of turtles live in North America. They eat different kinds of foods. But most turtles eat plants that grow in water. They may also eat small animals and fish.

Turtles make the best pets. They are beautiful and easy to care for. This may surprise you, but turtles are also friendly. They will swim across a pool to see you. Turtles are fun to watch, and they do not make much noise.

1. Which sentence is a fact?
   Ⓐ Turtles are friendly.
   Ⓑ The shell is hard and strong.
   Ⓒ Turtles are beautiful.

2. Which sentence is an opinion?
   Ⓐ Most turtles can pull their head and tail inside their shell.
   Ⓑ They do not make much noise.
   Ⓒ Turtles make the best pets.

Why I Love Trees

Trees are really tall, woody plants. Some trees have needles and are called "evergreens," while others have leaves instead.

A tree has only one stem, which is tall and covered with bark. A tree's roots grow deep into the ground. The roots suck up water and get minerals from the earth. The leaves or needles also take in sunlight. They use the sunlight, water, and minerals to make food for the tree.

Trees are wonderful. They help keep us cool in the summer and give us shade. It is great to take a nap under a tree.

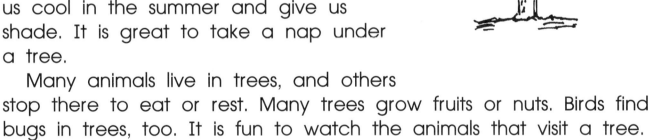

Many animals live in trees, and others stop there to eat or rest. Many trees grow fruits or nuts. Birds find bugs in trees, too. It is fun to watch the animals that visit a tree.

1. Which sentence is a fact?
 Ⓐ Trees are wonderful.
 Ⓑ It is great to nap under a tree.
 Ⓒ A tree has only one stem.

2. Which sentence from the passage is an opinion?
 Ⓐ "It is fun to watch the animals."
 Ⓑ "Some trees have needles."
 Ⓒ "A tree's roots grow deep into the ground."

Paul Bunyan and Babe

Paul Bunyan was taller than ten ordinary men, and he carried a big ax. Paul was a logger. He worked hard cutting down trees from Maine to California. People needed the trees for houses, wagons, and ships. The country was growing.

Paul loved his work, but sometimes he got a teeny bit lonely. Then one winter day he found a baby ox under a pile of snow. The ox was so cold it had turned blue. Paul named the ox Babe and took him home.

Babe grew into a giant-sized blue ox. He became a true friend to Paul Bunyan. When Paul cut down trees, Babe pulled the logs away. One time, Paul got upset about a logging road. That road was full of twists and turns. So Babe fixed it. He grabbed one end of the road in his teeth and pulled it out straight. He was a fine ox.

1. **What part of the story could not happen in real life?**
   Ⓐ Paul Bunyan carried an ax.
   Ⓑ He was taller than ten men.
   Ⓒ He worked hard cutting trees.

2. **What part of the story could happen in real life?**
   Ⓐ Babe grabbed a road in his teeth.
   Ⓑ Babe pulled the road straight.
   Ⓒ An ox pulled the logs away.

Ongoing Comprehension Strategy Assessment • 12

Name _____ Date _____

Directions: Read the passage. Then use the information from the passage to answer questions 1–2.

The Lion and the Mouse

One day long ago, a lion lay sleeping in the shade of the trees. He was having a very fine dream. But then a mouse ran across his paw and woke him up. The lion reached out and caught the mouse. He was about to eat the little creature when the mouse said, "Oh, please, great lion, don't eat me. Someday I might help you."

The lion thought this was funny. But he was in a good mood, so he let the mouse go.

A few days later, several hunters entered the woods. They caught the lion in a net and tied him down with ropes. Then they went off to get a wagon to carry the lion away.

While the hunters were gone, the mouse came by and saw the lion. Right away, he started to gnaw on the ropes. Very quickly, he chewed through the ropes and set the lion free.

"Thank you, my small friend," said the lion. "You did help me after all."

1. Which part of the story is make-believe?
 Ⓐ A lion was sleeping.
 Ⓑ The lion caught a mouse.
 Ⓒ A mouse talked to a lion.

2. What part of this story could happen in real life?
 Ⓐ A lion slept in the shade.
 Ⓑ A lion said, "Thank you."
 Ⓒ A mouse helped a lion.

Ants and Their Ways

Ants live in groups. A group of ants is called a colony. There are different kinds of ants in a colony. They help keep their group alive.

Most ants are workers. Their main job is to feed the group. They go out to find food. Some worker ants build the nest in the ground or in wood and keep the nest clean.

Other ants are fighters. They help keep the colony safe. Most ants can bite, and some have stingers they can use in a fight. Red fire ants can sting and bite.

In every group of ants, there is a queen. She is the mother of the colony. The queen rules the group and is much bigger than the others. She also lives longer. She lays thousands of eggs that later become workers, fighters, and new queens.

1. **What can you tell about ants from this passage?**
   Ⓐ The fighter ants are most important.
   Ⓑ Fighter ants do not need food.
   Ⓒ Ants have different jobs to do.

2. **The queen lays thousands of eggs. Most of these eggs become _____.**
   Ⓐ workers
   Ⓑ fighters
   Ⓒ queens

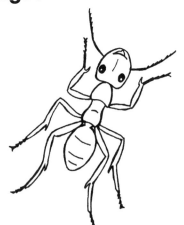

How Seeds Travel

Plants grow from seeds. The seeds need soil, water, and sunlight, and they need some room to grow. As plants grow, they make more seeds. Those new seeds must have their own places to grow.

How do seeds find places to grow? They travel in different ways.

Some seeds are very light. The wind blows them away. Some of the seeds land in good spots where they take root and grow.

Water also carries seeds. Seeds may fall into a river, and the river moves them along. When they float to land, the seeds can grow into new plants.

Animals also carry seeds. Some seeds hitch rides on an animal's coat until they fall off somewhere else. Many animals eat fruit with seeds inside. Birds eat seeds. They may fly off with seeds and drop some in different places. Squirrels bury nuts, which have seeds inside. The squirrels eat some of these nuts, but they leave others in the ground, where they grow into plants.

Do you like apples? Next time you eat one, look at the seeds. If you plant the seeds in a good place, they will grow.

1. What can you tell about seeds and animals from this passage?
  Ⓐ Animals carry seeds because they like to start new plants.
  Ⓑ Many kinds of animals carry seeds to new places.
  Ⓒ Animals should eat fewer seeds.

2. A "good place" to plant seeds has _____.
  Ⓐ wind
  Ⓑ animals
  Ⓒ soil, water, and sunlight

Name _____ Date _____

Directions: *Read the passage. Then use the information from the passage to answer questions 1–2.*

Tropical Fish Tanks

Tropical fish tanks take time to set up, and they are not cheap. But they are easy to keep up, and they're fun. Here's how to get started.

First, you have to decide on the size of your tank. It is best to begin with a ten-gallon tank. That's big enough for six to eight fish.

Next, fill the tank with clean water. Water from a sink is fine, but the water has to be clean. You will need to buy a small heater to keep the water warm enough for the fish. But the water cannot be too warm, and it cannot be too salty. You will need a filter to keep the water clean.

Fish also need places to sleep and hide. You can buy plants or a little cave or even a toy pirate ship at the store.

Now your tank is ready. You can pick out some fish. Goldfish are always good. Angelfish are pretty, and don't forget to buy a couple of suckers. They help keep the tank clean.

1. The author wrote this passage to _____.
Ⓐ make you want to get a fish tank
Ⓑ tell a funny story about fish
Ⓒ tell how to start a fish tank

2. What does the author think of fish tanks?
Ⓐ They are silly.
Ⓑ They are fun to have.
Ⓒ They cost too much money.

Sailing Ships

Airplanes have not been around very long. Even trains are fairly new. Just 200 years ago, traveling by water was the fastest way. People sailed across the ocean on ships.

These big ships had tall poles called masts, which held the sails. The sails were giant sheets made of canvas. Wind filled the sails and pushed the ship along. A trip could take a few weeks, or it could take much longer.

Giant sailing ships were like small towns. Sailors worked and lived on board. The work was hard, and the food was usually bad. The pay was low. The captain ran the ship. Some captains were mean and cruel, but many sailors did not mind. They liked going to new places, and they liked the freedom.

1. The author wrote this passage to _____.
    A give information about sailing ships
    B explain how to sail a ship
    C tell a funny story about a ship captain

2. What does the author think about a sailor's life?
    A A sailor had an easy life.
    B A sailor had a hard life, but it was exciting.
    C A sailor was lucky because he could make more money than a captain.

Name _____ Date _____

Directions: Read the passage. Then use the information from the passage to answer questions 1–2.

Germs

Germs are so small that you cannot see them, but they are everywhere. Many kinds of germs can make you sick. They cause colds and other illnesses.

Germs can spread in many ways. You can breathe in germs from the air. You can pick them up on money or trash, or another person may pass them to you. Germs can be found on food or animals, too.

But don't worry. Your body fights most germs and keeps you healthy. You can help fight against germs, too, by washing your hands. Wash before and after you eat. Wash after you use the bathroom and after you play outside. Washing your hands often will help get rid of unwanted germs.

1. The passage says that colds are caused by _____.
Ⓐ air
Ⓑ germs
Ⓒ animals

2. How can you help fight germs?
Ⓐ Wash your hands.
Ⓑ Go outside.
Ⓒ Stay home from school.

Name _____ Date _____

Directions: Read the passage. Then use the information from the passage to answer questions 1–2.

Making Bread

Have you ever made bread? It is not difficult to make, but it takes some time. Bread is made with flour and water. For most kinds of bread, you also need yeast. Yeast looks a little like sand, but it is alive.

First, mix the yeast in hot water. Then mix in the flour. Now you have some dough. Let the dough sit in a bowl in a warm place, and cover the bowl.

Before long, the dough will begin to rise, or grow. Why does this happen? The yeast causes the dough to puff up bigger and bigger. After a while, push down the dough and work in more flour. Then let the dough rise again. After a couple hours, you can bake it.

Why is bread soft? Yeast gives off gas bubbles which put air into the bread. The bubbles cause the bread to be soft. Without yeast, the bread stays flat and hard.

1. **What makes the bread soft?**
   Ⓐ gas bubbles from yeast
   Ⓑ fine, soft flour
   Ⓒ adding water

2. **What will happen if you make bread with only flour and water?**
   Ⓐ The bread will rise.
   Ⓑ The bread will be soft.
   Ⓒ The bread will be flat and hard.

Earthworms

Earthworms are simple creatures. They do not have eyes, a nose, or ears. They do not have bones or legs. It is hard for us to tell the head from the tail. On many kinds of worms, there is a light-colored band near the head, and the head has a mouth.

Earthworms are big eaters. They eat dead plants and animals, although they like some kinds of leaves more than others.

Even though they eat a lot, earthworms do not have teeth. Their food goes through their bodies and breaks down along the way. The leftovers come out the back end as "castings," which are very good for soil.

Earthworms are good for soil in another way. As they move through the earth looking for food, they act like little plows. They mix up the soil and make it loose.

1. What is the stated main idea of the first paragraph?
  Ⓐ Earthworms are simple creatures.
  Ⓑ They do not have eyes, nose, or ears.
  Ⓒ The head has a mouth.

2. How are earthworms good for the soil?
  Ⓐ They eat dead plants.
  Ⓑ They do not have teeth.
  Ⓒ They mix up soil and make it loose.

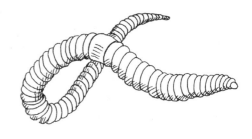

Buckle Up!

What should you do when you get in a car? You should put on your seat belt! It could save your life, and in most states you are required by law to wear a seat belt.

People make excuses for not using their seat belts. They say they are not going far, or their car is going slowly. But most accidents happen at slow speeds, and they happen near home. So put on your seat belt! Do not make excuses.

Other people say it takes too much time to put on a seat belt, or the seat belt does not feel good. Just practice. It will get faster as you get used to it. It feels much better than getting hurt. So put on your seat belt! Do not make excuses.

1. What is the stated main idea of this passage?
 Ⓐ Some people do not wear seat belts.
 Ⓑ In a car, you should put on your seat belt.
 Ⓒ Some people say it takes too much time.

2. Which is an excuse people give for not wearing a seat belt?
 Ⓐ I'm not going far.
 Ⓑ My car doesn't have one.
 Ⓒ I am too big.

How Cider Is Made

Fall is the best time for cider. You probably drink cider, but do you know where it comes from?

Cider comes from apples, and apples grow on trees. Picking apples is a lot of work. Some of the trees are tall, and the apples can be hard to reach. People pick the apples in the fall and send them to a cider mill.

Making cider takes a lot of apples. Big boxes of them come to the mill. The mill has a large machine called a cider press. First, the apples are washed. Then the press crushes the apples, and juice flows out. That is the cider. Workers pour the cider into big jugs.

People buy the jugs of cider and take them home. Some people drink their cider hot. Others like it cold. Hot or cold, cider tastes good!

1. What is the first thing you must do to make cider?
   Ⓐ Crush the apples.
   Ⓑ Wash the apples.
   Ⓒ Pick the apples.

2. What happens just after the apple juice flows out?
   Ⓐ Workers pour it into big jugs.
   Ⓑ It goes to the mill in big boxes.
   Ⓒ Workers wash the apples.

Mr. Willis and His Bricks

Have you ever seen a house made of bricks? Bricks come from the earth and are made from clay.

Mr. Willis likes to make bricks and use them to build things for his yard. First, he digs clay out of the ground. He likes red clay the best. Then he mixes the clay with water until it is like stiff mud. Next he mixes in some straw. The straw helps the bricks hold their shape when they are heated up.

He puts the clay into special boxes called molds. Mr. Willis lives in a very hot and sunny place. He puts the molds out in the sun to let the bricks dry. Then he takes the bricks out of the molds and lets them sit in the sun. The hot sun bakes them very dry and hard. If Mr. Willis lived in a rainy place, he would have to bake the bricks in a special oven called a kiln.

When the bricks are completely hard, Mr. Willis uses them to build low walls and paths in his yard. His friends and neighbors love the things he makes!

1. **What does Mr. Willis do before he mixes the clay with water?**
   Ⓐ He puts the clay into molds.
   Ⓑ He digs the clay out of the ground.
   Ⓒ He bakes it very hard and dry.

2. **What does Mr. Willis do after the bricks dry in the molds?**
   Ⓐ He mixes the clay with water.
   Ⓑ He mixes in some straw.
   Ⓒ He takes them out of the molds and bakes them in the sun.

Ongoing Comprehension Strategy Assessment • 23

Name _____ Date _____

Directions: Read the passage. Then use the information from the passage to answer questions 1–2.

A Special Day

"Tomorrow is a special day," said Mrs. Gordon to her second graders.
"Why is it special?" asked Lisa.
"Oh, you'll see," said Mrs. Gordon.
Later, all the children went outside. They sat under the big tree next to the school.
"Why do you think tomorrow is special?" asked Alex. "What day is it?"
The other kids shook their heads. "We don't know," they said.
Then Pablo's face lit up. "I bet I know!" he said. "I bet it's Mrs. Gordon's birthday!"
All the kids agreed. They decided to make birthday cards as a surprise.
The next day, Mrs. Gordon walked to her desk. As soon as she sat down, all the children shouted "HAPPY BIRTHDAY!" They took their cards out of their desks. Mrs. Gordon looked very surprised.
Just then Mr. Cook, the principal, came in. He held a big pile of books. "It's a special day, children," he said. "Did Mrs. Gordon tell you? Today is the day you get new reading books!"
All the children looked at Pablo. "Mrs. Gordon, it's not your birthday, is it?" said Pablo. Mrs. Gordon shook her head. "Oops," said Pablo.
Everyone laughed, even Mr. Cook.

1. Why did Mrs. Gordon look surprised when the children took out birthday cards?
   Ⓐ She thought they were in the wrong class.
   Ⓑ It wasn't really her birthday.
   Ⓒ The gifts were for Mr. Cook, not for her.

2. How did Pablo know he had made a mistake?
   Ⓐ Mr. Cook brought new books into the classroom.
   Ⓑ The children made cards for Mrs. Gordon.
   Ⓒ The other kids shook their heads.

Pretty as a Pearl

Pearls are pretty and round, like tiny white moons. They are used to make necklaces and other kinds of jewelry. Real pearls cost a lot of money. The only real pearls come from the sea.

Oysters are small sea creatures that live inside their shells. If little pieces of sand get inside the oysters' shells, it bothers them. They want to make the sand stop hurting. So they coat the bit of sand with a shiny layer of goo. They put many layers of goo around the sand. After a while the goo hardens like a shell. The oyster has made a pearl.

People love the way pearls look, but real pearls are rare. Divers swim down under the water. They find oysters and bring them back up to see if they have pearls in them. The divers have to work hard. It can take days to find one pearl.

Most pearls are white, but sometimes pearls come in colors. You can see pink pearls and some pearls the color of gold. No matter what color they are, they are always pretty.

1. Why do pearls cost a lot of money?
   Ⓐ They are made of gold.
   Ⓑ No one knows how they are made.
   Ⓒ They are hard to find.

2. Where do oysters live?
   Ⓐ inside pearls
   Ⓑ at the bottom of the sea
   Ⓒ in the sand

Directions: Read the passage. Then use the information from the passage to answer questions 1–2.

Monkey Business

In our country, cities have lots of birds that live on roofs and in trees. But in some parts of Asia, cities have monkeys. The monkeys live on roofs and in trees, too. Monkeys like the same food as people and will sometimes beg for food.

Monkeys are fun to watch. They are very strong, and they like to climb. They live with other monkeys in big families. Babies hold on to their mother's fur. That way they can be safe.

Monkeys like to play tricks. They like to jump and play. They are very curious and always want to know what's going on. Sometimes they steal food. If a group of monkeys get into your house, watch out!

1. If a group of monkeys gets into your house, what will probably happen?
Ⓐ They will clean your house.
Ⓑ They will hold on to each others' fur.
Ⓒ They will make a mess.

2. If some monkeys see you eating an ice cream cone, what will they probably do?
Ⓐ Run away.
Ⓑ Come and beg for some.
Ⓒ Hide behind you.

Name _____ Date _____

Directions: Read the passage. Then use the information from the passage to answer questions 1–2.

Jake's Tree House

One morning when Jake woke up, he had a wonderful idea. He would build a tree house! Jake asked his dad, "Is it okay if I build a tree house in the old oak?"

"It's not only okay," said Dad, "I'll even help you build it."

The two of them went out to the oak tree after breakfast and measured. Then they got some boards and started cutting with a saw. When the pieces were ready, Jake climbed up in the tree and Dad handed him the boards. Dad nailed them to some sturdy branches.

Jake and his dad worked all day. They even put a roof over the tree house so it would stay dry in the rain. They finally finished just before dark.

After dinner that night, Jake asked his brother Pete if he could borrow a sleeping bag.

"Sure," said Pete. "But can I come with you?"

Jake smiled as they both ran upstairs to get ready.

1. **What will probably happen next?**
   A) Jake and Pete will sleep in the tree house.
   B) Pete will help Jake finish the tree house.
   C) Jake will go to bed upstairs and fall asleep.

2. **What will happen later if it starts raining outside?**
   A) Jake and Pete will get wet.
   B) Jake and Pete will come inside.
   C) The boys will stay dry in the tree house.

Name _____ Date _____

Directions: Read the passage. Then use the information from the passage to answer questions 1–2.

Along the Nile

The Nile is a river in Africa. It is the longest river in the world. The Nile is 4,160 miles long. It flows from the mountains of East Africa to the sea.

People have lived beside the Nile for thousands of years. The people of ancient Egypt got their water from the Nile. They used the water for drinking and to grow food. The river was very important to them. Some of the first cities in the world were built next to the Nile.

All around the Nile, the land is very dry. It is mostly sand. But every summer, the rains come to the mountains. Then the river floods. The flood brings soil down from the mountains to the valley. The soil is good for farming. That is why trees and gardens grow in the Nile Valley.

Today, people still live beside the Nile River. It is still very important to them.

1. Which is the best summary of this passage?
Ⓐ The Nile River flows 4,160 miles. It goes from the mountains of East Africa through Egypt.
Ⓑ The Nile River in Egypt is the longest river in the world. People have lived beside the Nile for thousands of years.
Ⓒ The land near the Nile River in Egypt is very dry. Every summer, the rains come and the river floods.

2. "Some of the first cities in the world were built next to the Nile." Which sentence has the same meaning as the sentence above?
Ⓐ The biggest cities in the world were built next to the Nile.
Ⓑ First, the world's cities grew up next to the Nile River.
Ⓒ Some of the world's first cities began by the Nile.

Name _____ Date _____

Directions: Read the passage. Then use the information from the passage to answer questions 1–2.

Beetles

Think of all the kinds of animals, plants, and bugs in the world. If you could add them all together, you would have a huge number. Now think about this. One in every five is a beetle! There are more kinds of beetles than any other kind of bug or animal! You can see beetles everywhere.

All beetles begin as eggs. Then they grow into small worms. Before long, they change into beetles. Every beetle has six legs. It has a mouth that chews. Most beetles have wings. Most of them eat plants. Some beetles are helpful to us, but some are not.

Have you seen those little red bugs with black spots? Those are ladybird beetles. Most people call them ladybugs. People like to have ladybugs in their gardens. They eat other insects.

Japanese beetles are different. They are shiny green and brown. People do not like these beetles. They eat plant roots, flowers, and fruits.

1. The passage says, "People do not like these beetles. They eat plant roots, flowers, and fruits." Which sentence has the same meaning?
   Ⓐ People and beetles eat plant roots, flowers, and fruits they like.
   Ⓑ People do not like these beetles, plant roots, flowers, and fruits.
   Ⓒ People do not like these beetles because they eat flowers and fruits.

2. Which sentences are the best summary of this passage?
   Ⓐ Many people have gardens. People like to have beetles in their gardens.
   Ⓑ There are many kinds of beetles. Some are helpful, and some are not.
   Ⓒ Most bugs are beetles. Most worms become beetles.

How to Make "Bees"

One day, Lily said that she really enjoys eating bees. When the other children groaned, Lily laughed. She promised to bring some bees to school for everyone to eat.

The next day, Lily and her mom brought in a tray of "bees." Then she told how to make them. Everyone ate some of Lily's bees.

	**1.** Cut some pears in half.
	**2.** Make thin stripes on each piece of pear.
	**3.** Add "wings" made of thin cookies.
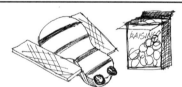	**4.** Make eyes for each bee.

1. What does Lily use to make the stripes?
  Ⓐ jelly
  Ⓑ orange peels
  Ⓒ chocolate sauce

2. What does Lily use to make the eyes?
  Ⓐ raisins
  Ⓑ stripes
  Ⓒ cookies

Name _____ Date _____

Directions: Read the passage. Then use the information from the passage to answer questions 1–2.

Animal Houses

Animals live in different kinds of houses. Many animals build their own houses. Birds build nests out of twigs and grass. Chipmunks dig holes to live in.

Other animals live in houses they find. Black bears live in holes or caves they find in the woods. A hermit crab looks for an empty shell. It makes a home in the shell. When the crab grows too big, it moves to a new shell.

Some animal houses don't look like houses to us. A spider web is made of thin threads. We can barely see it. But it is just right for a spider. Ants dig in the dirt to make tunnels. Many ants live together in one home.

Animal houses may be different. But every house is the right kind for the creature that lives there.

1. Where might a squirrel live?
   Ⓐ a hole in a tree
   Ⓑ a web
   Ⓒ an empty shell

2. Look at the pictures. Which animal house is made by people?
   Ⓐ the crab's shell
   Ⓑ the spider web
   Ⓒ the birdhouse

Did Your Clothes Grow?

You may know that many of your clothes are made in factories. But what are your clothes made from? Less than 100 years ago, all clothes were made from things that grow, such as plants, sheep, and even a special kind of worm! Today, many of the things you wear are made the same way.

Cotton • Cotton grows on a plant. The cotton looks like a puffy, white ball. It is picked and made into thread. People like to wear cotton in hot weather because it helps them stay cool.

Linen • Linen plants look like tall grass. They have blue flowers. The thread is strong. Sheets and clothes made from linen can last for many years.

Wool • Wool comes from sheep. It is very warm and makes soft yarn. It also makes strong thread for heavy coats. Wool is what people like to wear in winter.

Silk • Silk comes from silkworms. The worms make silk threads. The thread is very fine. Some people make very nice dresses and shirts out of silk.

1. Which part of the passage tells about a kind of plant?
   - Ⓐ Linen
   - Ⓑ Wool
   - Ⓒ Silk

2. Where does silk come from?
   - Ⓐ a plant
   - Ⓑ a kind of worm
   - Ⓒ sheep

Fun with Pine Cones

Every year, pine trees drop pine cones onto the ground. You can use those pine cones to make many fun things!

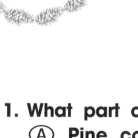

Pine cone bird feeder
Take a good-sized pine cone. Put peanut butter all over it. Then roll it in some birdseed. The seeds will stick to the peanut butter. Hang the pine cone outside. Birds will eat the seeds, and then they'll eat the peanut butter!

Pine cone holiday tree
Find a pine cone that is pointed at one end. Glue some cotton to the bottom of it. Then glue glitter to it and add some ribbon or beads.

Pine cone pets
Turn a pine cone on its side. Use glue and colored paper or pipe cleaners to make legs and tails. You can make dogs, mice, and cats. If you want, you can make up a monster for a pet!

Pine cone necklace
Find lots of tiny pine cones and ask an adult to help you thread a needle. Thread the pine cones together. Make a long string of them and tie the ends together. Now you can wear the pine cones as a necklace.

1. What part of the passage tells about making something to wear?
   - Ⓐ Pine cone bird feeder
   - Ⓑ Pine cone holiday tree
   - Ⓒ Pine cone necklace

2. What can you use to make legs and a tail on a pine cone pet?
   - Ⓐ pipe cleaners
   - Ⓑ ribbon and beads
   - Ⓒ thread

Name _____ Date _____

Directions: Read the passage. Then use the information from the passage to answer questions 1–2.

Sweeping to a Win

You probably know about baseball and football. But have you ever heard of curling?

Curling is a winter sport played by teams. It is played on ice. Players on each team toss big round stones across the ice. To keep the rocks moving, players sweep the ice. They use special brooms. The players are trying to get the stones to a target at the other end.

Curling is <u>easy</u> to learn, but it is hard to play. The stones are very heavy. It is difficult to send them where you want them to go. You must be <u>strong</u> to be good at curling.

Many countries have curling teams. More and more people want to play it. Maybe someday soon you will see a game of curling being played. Or maybe you will learn it yourself!

1. "Curling is <u>easy</u> to learn." Which word means the same as <u>easy</u>?
   Ⓐ hard
   Ⓑ light
   Ⓒ simple

2. "You must be <u>strong</u> to be good at curling." Which word means the OPPOSITE of <u>strong</u>?
   Ⓐ smart
   Ⓑ weak
   Ⓒ heavy

Name _____ Date _____

Directions: Read the passage. Then use the information from the passage to answer questions 1–2.

How to Be Healthy and Strong

Everyone wants to be healthy and strong. It is important to know how to get and stay <u>healthy</u>. There are three steps you should take.

The first step is to eat right. Many kids love candy and treats. But if that's all you ever eat, you will soon begin to feel ill. It is much better to eat fruit than candy bars, and try to eat vegetables at every meal. <u>Meat</u> and beans make you strong.

The second step is to exercise. It doesn't matter what you do as long as you move your body. You can dance or play tag, or you can run up a hill. You can even jump rope 100 times. Just get your body going! You will feel better for it.

The third step is to get plenty of sleep. It can be fun to stay up late once in a while. But if you do it all the time, you will start to feel tired even in the middle of the day. That's not fun, and it's not good for you. So make sure you get to sleep on time.

1. "Everyone wants to be <u>healthy</u>." Which word means the OPPOSITE of <u>healthy</u>?
   Ⓐ sick
   Ⓑ happy
   Ⓒ weak

2. "<u>Meat</u> and beans make you strong." In which of these sentences does the word <u>meat</u> fit in the blank?
   Ⓐ Dad plans to ____ us at the game.
   Ⓑ Did you ____ my friend Mena?
   Ⓒ Brian does not eat ____ or fish.

Name _____ Date _____

Directions: *Read the passage. Then use the information from the passage to answer questions 1–2.*

A World of Color

When you paint a picture, you may use many different colors. But where do the colors come from?

Long, long ago, people made paintings inside caves. They were made with colors dug from the ground. For example, red paint was made from red clay. Those paintings are thousands of years old. Today, the material for some paint colors is still dug out of the ground. Browns and dull yellows are often made from things in the earth.

Some colors are made with metals. Iron can make red, gold, and black. Cobalt makes a deep blue.

Other colors are made in a lab. Those colors are new. All paint is made with pigments. When you mix a pigment with oil, you get oil paint. Some artists make their own paint. They buy pigments. Then they combine the pigments with all kinds of things to make paint. They might use water, milk, or eggs. Mixing paints can be very messy, but it is fun, too!

1. "Cobalt makes a deep blue." What is cobalt?
   - Ⓐ a kind of metal
   - Ⓑ a type of brush
   - Ⓒ a famous place

2. "Then they combine the pigments." What clue helps you know that combine means "mix"?
   - Ⓐ "paint a picture"
   - Ⓑ "mixing paints"
   - Ⓒ "paintings inside caves"

Clowning Around

Some kids want to be pilots when they grow up. Some want to be doctors. But a few <u>fortunate</u> kids grow up to be clowns. They are the lucky ones!

How do you learn to be a clown? There are special schools just for clowns. When you go there, you learn everything you need to know. You learn to put on clown makeup. You make or buy clown costumes to wear. You learn silly tricks. Most important, you learn how to make people laugh.

Clowns use many kinds of tools and props. They have loud horns, funny wigs, and big glasses. They like to look as silly as they can. Sometimes clowns wear shoes that are so <u>gigantic</u> they trip over them!

Once a clown has finished clown school, he or she can work at a circus or a carnival. Some clowns work at birthday parties. Others visit sick kids to make them feel better. It's all in a day's work for a clown!

1. "Sometimes clowns wear shoes that are so **gigantic**." What does **gigantic** mean?
    Ⓐ well made
    Ⓑ bright red
    Ⓒ very large

2. "But a few **fortunate** kids grow up to be clowns." What clue helps you know that **fortunate** means "having good luck"?
    Ⓐ "They are the lucky ones!"
    Ⓑ "There are special schools just for clowns."
    Ⓒ "Most important, you learn how to make people laugh."

Your First Aquarium

Your mom won't let you get a dog, and your dad doesn't like cats. But you really want a pet. What can you do? Start an aquarium.

An aquarium is more than just a bowl of water with fish swimming around in it. It is a special place for fish to live <u>happily</u>. All you have to do is keep it clean and warm.

You can buy an aquarium and everything you need at a pet store. Then you can have fun choosing your fish. Some are very <u>colorful</u>, and some even seem to glow. Don't get too many fish, though. Fish don't like to be crowded. Also, don't feed your fish too often, because they don't know when to stop eating!

1. "It is a special place for fish to live <u>happily</u>." What does <u>happily</u> mean?
   - Ⓐ in a happy way
   - Ⓑ not happy
   - Ⓒ very happy

2. "Some are very <u>colorful</u>." What does <u>colorful</u> mean?
   - Ⓐ having no color
   - Ⓑ against color
   - Ⓒ filled with color

Good Queen Bess

Today, the ruler of England is Queen Elizabeth, the second. She is not the first queen with that name. A long time ago, there was another Queen Elizabeth. She was a great <u>leader</u>. The people of England loved her.

The first Elizabeth was known for her red hair. She liked to read and to dance. But she also knew how to get things done. In a war, her navy defeated Spain. Soon, England was the <u>strongest</u> country in the world.

Queen Elizabeth often wore fine dresses with pearls sewn all over them. She put gems in her hair. But she also loved to talk to her people. She traveled all over England visiting her people. They loved her for it. They called her "Good Queen Bess." To this day, the people of England remember her.

1. "She was a great <u>leader</u>."
   What does the word <u>leader</u> mean?
   Ⓐ in the lead
   Ⓑ without lead
   Ⓒ person who leads

2. "Soon, England was the <u>strongest</u> country in the world."
   The word <u>strongest</u> means —
   Ⓐ in a strong way
   Ⓑ most strong
   Ⓒ not strong

Midyear Test

Peace at Last 72

Native American Homes 74

A Gift for Mom 76

Teacher in a Barrel 78

Plants People Eat 80

On the Farm 82

An Animal Like No Other 84

1. A
2. B
3. B
4. C
5. A
6. C
7. B
8. B
9. A
10. C
11. C
12. A
13. A
14. C
15. C
16. B
17. B
18. C
19. B
20. A
21. A
22. C
23. A
24. B
25. C
26. B
27. A
28. C

Peace at Last

Once there was a man who was never happy. His children were too noisy. His home was too small and messy. He could never find any peace. "We need a bigger house!" he complained.

The family could not afford a bigger house, but the man's wife was wise. She came up with a plan.

First she went to the market to get a rooster. The rooster crowed from morning till night.

Next, the woman went to a farm to get a donkey. The donkey's hay made a mess all over.

Then the woman went to the zoo. This time she brought home an elephant, which filled an entire room. The family squeezed between the noisy rooster and the messy donkey.

"I can't stand this noisy, messy, crowded house another day!" cried the man.

His very wise wife took the rooster to market. She took the donkey back to the farm. Then she returned the elephant to the zoo. She cleaned the house from top to bottom.

"At last!" said the man. "Our home is clean. It feels so big and quiet. It's simply <u>amazing</u>!" From that day on, the man was content.

Name _____ Date _____

1. What does the woman bring home first?

   Ⓐ a rooster
   Ⓑ a horse
   Ⓒ an elephant

2. How does the man feel at the end of the story?

   Ⓐ tired
   Ⓑ happy
   Ⓒ worried

3. The story says, "It's simply amazing!" Which word means the same as amazing?

   Ⓐ busy
   Ⓑ surprising
   Ⓒ still

4. Which of these could NOT really happen?

   Ⓐ A man complains.
   Ⓑ A house seems crowded.
   Ⓒ An elephant lives in a house.

Midyear Test

Name _____ Date _____

Directions: Read the passage. Then use the information from the passage to answer questions 5–8.

Native American Homes

Long ago, Native Americans lived in different kinds of homes. The homes fit the way the people lived. They also fit where they lived.

People in forests lived in wigwams. These homes were round. Each home had a wood frame. It was covered with bark. These homes could be <u>built</u> quickly. They were good for people who moved in different seasons.

Longhouses were good for people who did not move. About 60 people could live in one longhouse.

Tepees were tents. They were shaped like cones. People placed hides over a wood frame. These made good homes on the wide open plains.

People on the plains moved often to hunt. They could take tepees down and set them up again fast.

In the desert, people lived in pueblos. These houses were made of mud bricks. The sun dried the mud. The thick walls kept out the heat.

Name _____ Date _____

5. What is the main idea of this passage?

   Ⓐ Native Americans lived in different kinds of houses.
   Ⓑ Most Native Americans lived in longhouses.
   Ⓒ Houses around the world are all alike.

6. Which people lived in tepees?

   Ⓐ people in the forests
   Ⓑ people in hot places
   Ⓒ people on the plains

7. The passage says, "These homes could be <u>built</u> quickly." What does <u>built</u> mean?

   Ⓐ broken
   Ⓑ made
   Ⓒ cleaned

8. The author wrote this passage to _____.

   Ⓐ show that people liked to move often
   Ⓑ describe different kinds of homes from the past
   Ⓒ tell a funny story about Native Americans

A Gift for Mom

It was Thursday. Mom's birthday was just one day away. Li dumped his piggy bank out on his bed. "Fourteen, fifteen, twenty-five, a dollar." He counted out seven dollars and 75 cents.

Li walked to the pet store. A cute puppy stared at him through the window. Li looked at the sign. The puppy cost too much.

On his way home, Li passed a sign. It said, "Puppies for sale." Li knocked on the door. A cute puppy wagged his tail. "How much?" asked Li. The woman told him. It was much too much.

Li passed by a pet shelter. He went in to see the dogs and cats. A cute puppy jumped up and licked his face. "How much?" he asked the worker.

"It's free to a good home," said the man.

Li said, "I'll take it. I'll take a bowl and a leash, too, please." He pulled his money from his pocket and proudly paid the man.

Name _____ Date _____

9. What will happen next in the story?

  Ⓐ Li will give the puppy to his mother.
  Ⓑ Li will try to earn some more money.
  Ⓒ Li will try to sell the puppy.

10. What problem does Li have at first?

  Ⓐ His father does not have money for a present.
  Ⓑ His mother does not want a dog.
  Ⓒ Li does not have enough money to buy a dog.

11. What does Li pay for?

  Ⓐ a piggy bank
  Ⓑ a new puppy
  Ⓒ a bowl and a leash

12. The author's purpose in this passage is to _____.

  Ⓐ tell a story about a boy and his family
  Ⓑ make children want to save money
  Ⓒ describe the best kind of dog to own

Directions: Read the passage. Then use the information from the passage to answer questions 13–16.

Teacher in a Barrel

In 1901, Annie Edson Taylor turned 63 years old. She was a teacher and needed to earn money. Annie did something amazing. She went over a huge waterfall called Niagara Falls in a pickle barrel.

No one had ever done that safely before. Few people have done it since.

Annie stepped into the barrel. Her helper put a lid on it. Then he pumped in air. That helped Annie breathe.

The barrel dropped about 170 feet into the river below. Annie bumped her head and got a cut. Aside from that, she was okay. Annie climbed out down the river 17 minutes later. She had done it!

Annie told people that no one should ever try that again. She was right. It was foolish to try something so risky.

Reporters took pictures and wrote about Annie. She gave speeches. Sadly, she never did earn much money from her dangerous stunt.

Name _____ Date _____

13. This passage mostly tells about _____.

- Ⓐ events in time order
- Ⓑ two things that are alike
- Ⓒ how to make something

14. Which sentence is an opinion?

- Ⓐ Annie was a teacher.
- Ⓑ Annie went over the falls in a barrel.
- Ⓒ Annie did a very foolish thing.

15. What can you tell about Annie Edson Taylor?

- Ⓐ She enjoyed swimming.
- Ⓑ She was a good teacher.
- Ⓒ She was a brave person.

16. What does <u>helper</u> mean?

- Ⓐ help again
- Ⓑ someone who helps
- Ⓒ a place for helping

Name _____ Date _____

Directions: Read the passage. Then use the information from the passage to answer questions 17–20.

Plants People Eat

Vegetables are plants that people eat. What part of each plant can you eat? On some plants, you may eat the roots, stems, or leaves. On others, you may eat the seeds or the fruit instead.

Roots in the Ground

Roots grow under the ground. Plants use their roots to get water. Potatoes and carrots are root vegetables.

The Middle Parts

Stalks, or stems, are the middle parts of the plant. The stem carries food and water to the leaves. Do you like celery? That's a stem vegetable.

Leaves

Leaves make food for plants in bright sunshine. Lettuce is a leafy vegetable. So is kale.

Fruits and Seeds

The flowers on vegetables turn into fruit. Do you like squash or tomatoes? Those are the fruit parts of the plants. Beans and peas are actually seeds.

The chart shows parts of some other plants we eat.

Vegetable	Root	Stem	Leaf	Fruit
spinach			✔	
beet	✔			
asparagus		✔		
cucumber				✔

Name _____ Date _____

17. Which is the best summary of this passage?

- Ⓐ People should eat vegetables. Green plants are healthy foods.
- Ⓑ People eat different parts of plants. They eat roots, stems, leaves, and fruit.
- Ⓒ Carrots and potatoes are root vegetables. These parts grow in the ground.

18. Which part of the passage tells how plants get water?

- Ⓐ **Leaves**
- Ⓑ **The Middle Parts**
- Ⓒ **Roots in the Ground**

19. What part of an asparagus plant do people eat?

- Ⓐ root
- Ⓑ stem
- Ⓒ leaf

20. Which of these vegetables is a leaf?

- Ⓐ spinach
- Ⓑ broccoli
- Ⓒ corn

Midyear Test

Name _____ Date _____

Directions: Read the passage. Then use the information from the passage to answer questions 21–24.

On the Farm

"Yay, it's summer!" shouted Red. Her cousin Ted was coming to visit the next day. She couldn't wait to show him the farm.

When Ted got there, Red said, "Let's go swim in the pond."

"I can't swim," said Ted.

"Let's go ride horses," said Red.

"I can't ride," said Ted.

"Let's go drive a tractor," suggested Red.

"What's a tractor?" said Ted.

Red was running out of ideas. She asked Ted, "What do you do in the city? How do you have fun?"

Ted said, "We play in the park. I go to museums with my mom. I have play dates. Sometimes we go to the farmer's market."

"Let's go pick peaches," said Red. "Maybe my dad will make a pie. He makes great peach pie."

"Peach pie is my favorite!" said Ted. "Just show me where to start!"

Name _____ Date _____

21. What was Red's first idea in this story?

Ⓐ to go swimming with Ted
Ⓑ to ride horses with Ted
Ⓒ to pick peaches with Ted

22. What was something Ted did not know about?

Ⓐ having a play date
Ⓑ going to a museum
Ⓒ driving a tractor

23. How are Ted and Red alike?

Ⓐ They both like peaches.
Ⓑ They both play in a park.
Ⓒ They both like to swim.

24. Red was running out of ideas because _____.

Ⓐ Ted wanted to pick peaches
Ⓑ Ted did not know about life on a farm
Ⓒ Ted wanted to stay in the city and see his friends

An Animal Like No Other

Is it a duck or a beaver? A duck-billed platypus is like many animals in some ways. It is also a <u>creature</u> like no other.

A platypus has a bill like a duck. It likes to eat worms. It often scoops food from mud with its bill.

It has a smooth, flat tail like a beaver. The tail is a good tool for swimming.

The platypus has a soft, thick fur coat. It looks like an otter.

This animal is cute. It is also dangerous, like some snakes. Males have sharp claws on their feet. These claws have poison in them. They can really hurt!

The platypus is a kind of mammal, like dogs and people. The babies are born with hair or fur. The mother feeds the babies milk, like other mammals do. But unlike other mammals, platypus babies come from eggs.

Name _____ Date _____

25. How is a duck-billed platypus like a beaver?

Ⓐ A platypus lays eggs.
Ⓑ A platypus has sharp claws.
Ⓒ A platypus has a flat tail.

26. Which sentence is a fact?

Ⓐ A platypus is cute.
Ⓑ A platypus is a mammal.
Ⓒ A platypus is funny-looking.

27. The passage says, "But unlike other mammals, platypus babies come from eggs." Which sentence has the same meaning?

Ⓐ A platypus comes from an egg, but other mammals don't.
Ⓑ A platypus has babies, just like other kinds of mammals.
Ⓒ Many animals come from eggs.

28. The passage says, "It is a <u>creature</u> like no other." What does <u>creature</u> mean?

Ⓐ tail
Ⓑ food
Ⓒ animal

Posttest

The Mule and the Horse 88

A Walk on the Moon 90

The Sandwich Switch 92

The Boy Who Loved Snow 94

Our Solar System 96

At the Dentist 98

Bats 100

Posttest Answer Key

1. B
2. C
3. A
4. B
5. C
6. B
7. C
8. A
9. A
10. C
11. A
12. B
13. A
14. C
15. C
16. B
17. A
18. B
19. B
20. A
21. B
22. C
23. A
24. A
25. B
26. C
27. B
28. C

The Mule and the Horse

A farmer had a mule and a horse. One day the farmer filled some baskets with corn. He tied some of the baskets to the horse and tied the rest to the mule. Then he led the animals along the road to the market.

Soon they came to a steep hill. The mule went up the hill quickly, but the horse slowed to a stop. "I need help," the horse told the mule. "Please take part of my load."

"No, I won't," said the mule. "My load is heavy enough."

The horse took a few more steps, but then it slipped and fell. With that, the farmer took the baskets from the horse's back. He tied them to the mule and started off again for the market, leaving the horse to rest beside the road.

"What a fool I am," the mule thought. "I would not give the horse a little help, and now I must carry the whole load myself."

Name _____ Date _____

1. Where does this story take place?
   Ⓐ in a cornfield
   Ⓑ on a road
   Ⓒ at a market

2. Which word best describes the mule in this story?
   Ⓐ clever
   Ⓑ weak
   Ⓒ selfish

3. In the story, the mule says, "My load is heavy enough." Which word means the *opposite* of heavy?
   Ⓐ light
   Ⓑ big
   Ⓒ new

4. Which part of this story could NOT really happen?
   Ⓐ A horse and a mule carry baskets of corn.
   Ⓑ The horse asks the mule for help.
   Ⓒ The horse slips and falls.

Posttest

Name _____ Date _____

Directions: Read the passage. Then use the information from the passage to answer questions 5–8.

A Walk on the Moon

On July 16, 1969, a spaceship blasted off from Earth. The spaceship was called Apollo 11. Three men were on the ship: Neil Armstrong, Buzz Aldrin, and Michael Collins. They were going to the moon.

Four days later, Apollo 11 was near the moon. Two men left the ship in a small craft and landed on the moon. Neil Armstrong <u>emerged</u> first. Then Buzz Aldrin followed. They walked on the moon. The walk was shown on TV. People watched around the world. It was a big day.

The men picked up moon rocks and took pictures. They left a U.S. flag. Then they returned to Apollo 11 and headed home.

They got back to Earth four days later. They were heroes. They soon rode in a parade. Everybody wanted to see them.

Name _____ Date _____

5. **What is the main idea of this passage?**
   Ⓐ The spaceship was called Apollo 11.
   Ⓑ They left a U.S. flag on the moon.
   Ⓒ Three men went to the moon in 1969.

6. **What did Armstrong and Aldrin do on the moon?**
   Ⓐ They left Apollo 11 in a small craft for four days.
   Ⓑ They, walked, picked up rocks, and took pictures.
   Ⓒ They rode in a parade for everybody to see.

7. **The passage says, "Neil Armstrong <u>emerged</u> first." What does <u>emerged</u> mean?**
   Ⓐ hit hard
   Ⓑ talked
   Ⓒ got out

8. **The author wrote this passage to _____.**
   Ⓐ tell about a trip to the moon
   Ⓑ compare the moon and Earth
   Ⓒ tell a funny story about spaceships

The Sandwich Switch

Nell could hardly wait for the lunch bell to ring. Her stomach had been growling all morning. When Ms. Jacobs told the students to line up, Nell was first in line. She walked as quickly as she could to the lunchroom.

Nell unzipped her lunch bag and took out the sandwich. As she unwrapped it, she gasped. "Oh, no!" cried Nell. "I've got Carl's lunch!"

"What are you talking about?" asked Nell's friend, Wendy.

"Mom must have switched our sandwiches by mistake this morning," Nell explained. "Carl must have my peanut butter sandwich, because I've got his tuna fish!"

"So what's the big deal?" replied Wendy. "Just eat Carl's sandwich today."

Nell made a face and said, "But I don't like tuna fish! It's too smelly! I never eat it!"

Wendy nodded her head. "You're right about the smell," she said. "But tuna fish actually tastes pretty good. Just take a bite and you'll see."

With one hand, Nell covered her nose. With the other, she raised the sandwich to her mouth and took a bite. She chewed slowly and then swallowed.

Wendy watched Nell closely. "Well, what do you think?" she asked.

Nell smiled and said, "Not too bad at all."

Name _____ Date _____

9. **What will happen next in the story?**
   - Ⓐ Nell will finish the tuna fish sandwich.
   - Ⓑ Wendy will eat Nell's sandwich.
   - Ⓒ Nell will buy a school lunch.

10. **What is the problem in this story?**
    - Ⓐ Nell's class is late for lunch.
    - Ⓑ Wendy plays a trick on Nell.
    - Ⓒ Nell brings the wrong lunch to school.

11. **Who is Carl in this story?**
    - Ⓐ Nell's brother
    - Ⓑ a boy in Nell's class
    - Ⓒ Nell's neighbor

12. **The author's purpose in this passage is to _____.**
    - Ⓐ teach that tuna fish is healthful to eat
    - Ⓑ tell a funny story about Nell
    - Ⓒ explain how to make a sandwich

Directions: Read the passage. Then use the information from the passage to answer questions 13–16.

The Boy Who Loved Snow

Wilson Bentley was born in 1865. He grew up on a farm in Vermont. His mother taught him to read and write. His father taught him to farm.

Vermont has awful winters. They are cold and snowy. But Wilson loved winter. He loved to play in the snow. He loved to look at it, too.

When he was fifteen, Wilson got a gift. It was a microscope. He used it to look at snowflakes. He could not believe his eyes! Each one had six sides, but each one was special. No two snowflakes were alike.

Wilson started drawing snowflakes. He drew 400 flakes in all, but the job was hard. The flakes melted quickly. Wilson was <u>unhappy</u> with the drawings.

Then Wilson bought a special camera. It could take pictures of tiny things. Wilson started taking pictures of snowflakes. He kept taking them for the rest of his life.

In 1931, Wilson Bentley published a book of his pictures. He was very proud of his work. But he died a few weeks later. He was sixty-six years old.

Name _____ Date _____

13. This passage mostly tells about _____.
- Ⓐ events in time order
- Ⓑ how two things are alike
- Ⓒ how to do something

14. Which sentence is an opinion?
- Ⓐ Wilson Bentley was born in 1865.
- Ⓑ He grew up on a farm in Vermont.
- Ⓒ Vermont has awful winters.

15. What can you tell about Wilson from this passage?
- Ⓐ He liked taking pictures of people.
- Ⓑ He became a great artist.
- Ⓒ He never got tired of snowflakes.

16. The passage says, "Wilson was <u>unhappy</u> with the drawings." What does <u>unhappy</u> mean?
- Ⓐ make happy
- Ⓑ not happy
- Ⓒ happy again

Posttest

Name _____ Date _____

Directions: Read the passage. Then use the information from the passage to answer questions 17–20.

Our Solar System

What is the solar system? It is made up of the sun and the planets that move around it. Earth is one of those planets. Let's find out more about the solar system.

The Sun

The sun is a star much like any star in the sky. It is a ball of burning gas. But our sun is special in one way. It is much closer to us than any other star. Many stars are much bigger than the sun. But the sun looks huge because it is so close.

The Planets

There are eight planets in our solar system. All of them move around the sun. But the planets are different in many ways. Some are made mostly of rock. Others are made of gas. Some are very hot, but others are very cold.

Here's another way the planets are different. Some have moons, but some do not. This chart shows how many moons each planet has.

Name of Planet	Number of Moons
Mercury	0
Venus	0
Earth	1
Mars	2
Jupiter	63
Saturn	31
Uranus	27
Neptune	13

Name _____ Date _____

17. Which sentence best summarizes the passage?
  Ⓐ In our solar system, eight planets move around the sun.
  Ⓑ Some of the eight planets in our solar system have moons.
  Ⓒ Earth and the sun are always moving.

18. Which part of the passage tells how the sun is different from other stars?
  Ⓐ **The Planets**
  Ⓑ **The Sun**
  Ⓒ the chart

19. Which planets do not have any moons?
  Ⓐ Jupiter and Mars
  Ⓑ Venus and Mercury
  Ⓒ Saturn and Earth

20. How many moons does Neptune have?
  Ⓐ 13
  Ⓑ 27
  Ⓒ 31

At the Dentist

Today Ben, Tyler, and I went to the dentist. It was time to get our teeth cleaned. Ben and I have been to the dentist many times. We weren't worried. But this was Tyler's first visit, and he was afraid.

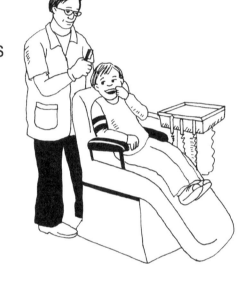

Dr. Huber met us in the waiting room. "Who's first?" he asked.

"NOT ME!" Tyler said loudly.

Mom whispered something to Dr. Huber. He nodded and said, "He'll be fine." Then he added, "We'll go from oldest to youngest. Come along, Ellie."

When Dr. Huber finished cleaning my teeth, he showed me the prize box. I started to take a jump rope, but then I got a great idea. I reached for a toy car instead. I walked out to the waiting room and sat down next to Tyler.

"Boy, that was fun," I said to him. "Dr. Huber cleaned my teeth with bubble gum flavored toothpaste, and then he gave me this toy car for a prize!"

Just then Dr. Huber appeared again. "Okay," he began. "Ellie's finished. Now it's Ben's turn."

That's when Tyler jumped out of his seat and hurried over to Dr. Huber. "Let me go next, please, please!" he said.

Dr. Huber laughed and said, "Sure, Tyler, let's go."

Name _____ Date _____

21. Whose teeth did Dr. Huber clean first?
- Ⓐ Ben's
- Ⓑ Ellie's
- Ⓒ Tyler's

22. Why did Ellie take the toy car?
- Ⓐ It was the best prize in the box.
- Ⓑ She liked playing with toy cars.
- Ⓒ She knew Tyler would like it.

23. How was Tyler different from Ellie?
- Ⓐ He had never been to the dentist before.
- Ⓑ He did not like prizes.
- Ⓒ He liked bubble gum toothpaste.

24. What happened when Tyler saw the toy car?
- Ⓐ He asked Dr. Huber to let him go next.
- Ⓑ He started to get worried.
- Ⓒ He asked to look at the prize box.

Posttest

Name _____ Date _____

Directions: Read the passage. Then use the information from the passage to answer questions 25–28.

Bats

Bats are amazing creatures. Like birds, they have wings and can fly. But in most other ways, bats aren't at all like birds. They don't lay eggs, they don't build nests, and they don't have feathers. Instead, a bat has fur. From up close, a bat <u>resembles</u> a mouse with wings.

So what are bats, exactly? They belong to the animal group called mammals. Mice, squirrels, and dogs are mammals, and so are elephants and humans. Any animal with fur or hair is a mammal. But bats are the only mammals that fly.

Some people are afraid of bats. They think a bat will bite them, but bats are shy. They mostly stay away from people. Bats sleep all day long and come out at night to eat. Their main food is insects. Bats eat many insects that bother people. In this way, bats help us.

Name _____ Date _____

25. How are bats like birds?
 Ⓐ They build nests.
 Ⓑ They can fly.
 Ⓒ They lay eggs.

26. Which sentence is a fact?
 Ⓐ Bats are amazing creatures.
 Ⓑ Bats are scary.
 Ⓒ Bats sleep in the day.

27. Which is the best summary of this passage?
 Ⓐ Animals with feathers are mammals. Bats are flying mammals.
 Ⓑ Bats are flying mammals. They are more helpful than people think.
 Ⓒ Animals with fur are mammals. Some mammals can fly.

28. The passage says, "From up close, a bat resembles a mouse with wings." What does resembles mean?
 Ⓐ lives near
 Ⓑ needs
 Ⓒ looks like

Answer Sheet

Student Name _____ Date _____

Teacher Name _____ Grade _____

Pretest   **Midyear Test**   **Posttest**

(Circle one.)

1. Ⓐ Ⓑ Ⓒ Ⓓ   15. Ⓐ Ⓑ Ⓒ Ⓓ
2. Ⓐ Ⓑ Ⓒ Ⓓ   16. Ⓐ Ⓑ Ⓒ Ⓓ
3. Ⓐ Ⓑ Ⓒ Ⓓ   17. Ⓐ Ⓑ Ⓒ Ⓓ
4. Ⓐ Ⓑ Ⓒ Ⓓ   18. Ⓐ Ⓑ Ⓒ Ⓓ
5. Ⓐ Ⓑ Ⓒ Ⓓ   19. Ⓐ Ⓑ Ⓒ Ⓓ
6. Ⓐ Ⓑ Ⓒ Ⓓ   20. Ⓐ Ⓑ Ⓒ Ⓓ
7. Ⓐ Ⓑ Ⓒ Ⓓ   21. Ⓐ Ⓑ Ⓒ Ⓓ
8. Ⓐ Ⓑ Ⓒ Ⓓ   22. Ⓐ Ⓑ Ⓒ Ⓓ
9. Ⓐ Ⓑ Ⓒ Ⓓ   23. Ⓐ Ⓑ Ⓒ Ⓓ
10. Ⓐ Ⓑ Ⓒ Ⓓ   24. Ⓐ Ⓑ Ⓒ Ⓓ
11. Ⓐ Ⓑ Ⓒ Ⓓ   25. Ⓐ Ⓑ Ⓒ Ⓓ
12. Ⓐ Ⓑ Ⓒ Ⓓ   26. Ⓐ Ⓑ Ⓒ Ⓓ
13. Ⓐ Ⓑ Ⓒ Ⓓ   27. Ⓐ Ⓑ Ⓒ Ⓓ
14. Ⓐ Ⓑ Ⓒ Ⓓ   28. Ⓐ Ⓑ Ⓒ Ⓓ

Individual Pretest Scoring Chart

Student Name _____ Date _____

Teacher Name _____ Grade _____

Skill Cluster Comprehension or Word Study Strategy	Item Numbers	Pretest Score
1 Literary Elements Analyze Character Analyze Story Elements Distinguish Real from Make-Believe	1, 2, 4, 10	/4
2 Text Structure and Features Analyze Text Structure and Organization Use Graphic Features Use Text Features	13, 18, 19, 20	/4
3 Relating Ideas Compare and Contrast Identify Cause and Effect Identify Sequence of Events	21, 23, 24, 25	/4
4 Inferences and Conclusions Draw Conclusions Make Inferences Make Predictions	9, 11, 15, 22	/4
5 Making Judgments Evaluate Fact and Opinion Evaluate Author's Purpose	8, 12, 14, 26	/4
6 Distinguishing Important Information Identify Main Idea and Supporting Details Summarize Information	5, 6, 17, 27	/4
7 Word Study Identify Synonyms, Antonyms, and Homonyms Use Context Clues to Determine Word Meaning Use Word Structures to Determine Word Meaning	3, 7, 16, 28	/4
Total		/28
Percent Score		___%

Individual Midyear Test Scoring Chart

Student Name _____ Date _____

Teacher Name _____ Grade _____

Skill Cluster Comprehension or Word Study Strategy	Item Numbers	Midyear Score

1 **Literary Elements**
    Analyze Character
    Analyze Story Elements
    Distinguish Real from Make-Believe
	1, 2, 4, 10	/4

2 **Text Structure and Features**
    Analyze Text Structure and Organization
    Use Graphic Features
    Use Text Features
	13, 18, 19, 20	/4

3 **Relating Ideas**
    Compare and Contrast
    Identify Cause and Effect
    Identify Sequence of Events
	21, 23, 24, 25	/4

4 **Inferences and Conclusions**
    Draw Conclusions
    Make Inferences
    Make Predictions
	9, 11, 15, 22	/4

5 **Making Judgments**
    Evaluate Fact and Opinion
    Evaluate Author's Purpose
	8, 12, 14, 26	/4

6 **Distinguishing Important Information**
    Identify Main Idea and Supporting Details
    Summarize Information
	5, 6, 17, 27	/4

7 **Word Study**
    Identify Synonyms, Antonyms, and Homonyms
    Use Context Clues to Determine Word Meaning
    Use Word Structures to Determine Word Meaning
	3, 7, 16, 28	/4

Total		/28
Percent Score		___%

Individual Posttest Scoring Chart

Student Name _____ Date _____

Teacher Name _____ Grade _____

Skill Cluster Comprehension or Word Study Strategy	Item Numbers	Posttest Score
1 Literary Elements Analyze Character Analyze Story Elements Distinguish Real from Make-Believe	1, 2, 4, 10	/4
2 Text Structure and Features Analyze Text Structure and Organization Use Graphic Features Use Text Features	13, 18, 19, 20	/4
3 Relating Ideas Compare and Contrast Identify Cause and Effect Identify Sequence of Events	21, 23, 24, 25	/4
4 Inferences and Conclusions Draw Conclusions Make Inferences Make Predictions	9, 11, 15, 22	/4
5 Making Judgments Evaluate Fact and Opinion Evaluate Author's Purpose	8, 12, 14, 26	/4
6 Distinguishing Important Information Identify Main Idea and Supporting Details Summarize Information	5, 6, 17, 27	/4
7 Word Study Identify Synonyms, Antonyms, and Homonyms Use Context Clues to Determine Word Meaning Use Word Structures to Determine Word Meaning	3, 7, 16, 28	/4
Total		/28
Percent Score		___%

©2015 Benchmark Education Company, LLC

Group Pretest/Midyear Test/Posttest Comparison Chart

Teacher Name _____ Grade _____

Student Name	Pretest		Midyear Test		Posttest	
	Total Correct	Percent Score	Total Correct	Percent Score	Total Correct	Percent Score

Ongoing Strategy Assessment Record

Student Name _____ Date _____

Teacher Name _____ Grade _____

No.	Comprehension or Word Study Strategy	Reading or Listening		Reading or Listening	
		Date of 1st Assessment	Score	Date of 2nd Assessment	Score
1–2	Analyze Character				
3–4	Analyze Story Elements				
5–6	Analyze Text Structure and Organization				
7–8	Compare and Contrast				
9–10	Evaluate Fact and Opinion				
11–12	Distinguish Real from Make-Believe				
13–14	Draw Conclusions				
15–16	Evaluate Author's Purpose				
17–18	Identify Cause and Effect				
19–20	Identify Main Idea and Supporting Details				
21–22	Identify Sequence of Events				
23–24	Make Inferences				
25–26	Make Predictions				
27–28	Summarize Information				
29–30	Use Graphic Features				
31–32	Use Text Features				
33–34	Identify Synonyms, Antonyms, and Homonyms				
35–36	Use Context Clues to Determine Word Meaning				
37–38	Use Word Structures to Determine Word Meaning				

Common Core State Standards and Virginia SOL Correlations

Pretest			Midyear Test			Posttest		
Item	CCSS	VA SOL	Item	CCSS	VA SOL	Item	CCSS	VA SOL
1.	RL.2.1	2.8c, 2.8 CF	1.	RL.2.3	2.8 CF	1.	RL.2.3	2.8c, 2.8 CF
2.	RL.2.3	2.8 CF	2.	RL.2.3	2.8h	2.	RL.2.3	2.8 CF
3.	RL.2.4	2.7a, 2.7c	3.	RL.2.4	2.8h	3.	RL.2.4	2.7a, 2.7c
4.	RL.2.1	2.8c	4.	RL.2.1	2.8c	4.	RL.2.1	2.8c
5.	RI.2.2	2.9g	5.	RI.2.2	2.9g	5.	RI.2.2	2.9g
6.	RI.2.2	2.9g, 2.9 CF	6.	RI.2.1	2.9e	6.	RI.2.3	2.9g, 2.9 CF
7.	RI.2.4	2.7 CF	7.	RI.2.4	2.7 CF	7.	RI.2.4	2.7 CF
8.	RI.2.6	2.9d, 2.9g	8.	RI.2.6	2.9d, 2.9g	8.	RI.2.6	2.9d, 2.9g
9.	RL.2.1	2.8a, 2.8i	9.	RL.2.1	2.8c, 2.8 CF	9.	RL.2.1	2.8a, 2.8i
10.	RL.2.2	2.8c, 2.8 CF	10.	RL.2.3	2.8 CF	10.	RL.2.3	2.8c, 2.8 CF
11.	RL.2.1	2.8c, 2.8i	11.	RL.2.1	2.8c, 2.8 CF	11.	RL.2.1	2.8c, 2.8i
12.	RL.2.6	2.1 CF	12.	RL.2.6	2.7a, 2.7c	12.	RL.2.6	2.1 CF
13.	RI.2.5	2.10b, 2.10c	13.	RI.2.2	2.9g	13.	RI.2.2	2.10b, 2.10c
14.	RI.2.8	2.9 CF	14.	RI.2.8	2.9 CF	14.	RI.2.8	2.9 CF
15.	RI.2.1	2.9e	15.	RI.2.1	2.9e	15.	RI.2.1	2.9e
16.	RI.2.4	2.7 CF	16.	RI.2.4	2.7 CF	16.	RI.2.4	2.7 CF
17.	RI.2.2	2.9g	17.	RI.2.2	2.9g	17.	RI.2.2	2.9g
18.	RI.2.5	2.9 CF, 2.10b	18.	RI.2.5	2.9 CF, 2.10b	18.	RI.2.5	2.9 CF, 2.10b
19.	RI.2.4	2.7 CF	19.	RI.2.7	2.9 CF	19.	RI.2.7	2.9 CF
20.	RI.2.7	2.9 CF	20.	RI.2.7	2.9 CF	20.	RI.2.7	2.9 CF
21.	RL.2.3	2.8 CF	21.	RL.2.3	2.8 CF	21.	RL.2.1	2.8c, 2.8 CF
22.	RL.2.1	2.8c, 2.8i	22.	RL.2.1	2.8 CF	22.	RL.2.1	2.8c, 2.8i
23.	RL.2.3	2.8 CF	23.	RL.2.3	2.8 CF	23.	RL.2.3	2.8 CF
24.	RL.2.3	2.8 CF	24.	RL.2.3	2.8 CF	24.	RL.2.3	2.8 CF
25.	RI.2.3	2.9 CF	25.	RI.2.3	2.9 CF	25.	RI.2.3	2.9 CF
26.	RI.2.8	2.9 CF	26.	RI.2.1	2.9e	26.	RI.2.8	2.9 CF
27.	RI.2.4	2.7 CF, 2.9g	27.	RI.2.1	2.9e, 2.9f	27.	RI.2.2	2.9g, 2.9 CF
28.	RI.2.4	2.7 CF	28.	RI.2.4	2.7 CF, 2.9e, 2.9f	28.	RI.2.4	2.7 CF

Notes

Notes

Notes

Notes